AF802961

PENGUIN BUSINESS

FINANCIAL AFFAIRS OF THE COMMON MAN

Anil Lamba is a bestselling author, financial literacy activist and an international corporate trainer. He is a chartered accountant who holds degrees in commerce and law, as well as a doctorate in taxation. His training programmes are held internationally, with a client list exceeding 2000 large- and medium-sized corporations across India, the US, Europe, Russia, Africa, the Middle East and the Far East.

A pioneer in the field of distance education, he has created several series of blended e-learning and training videos on finance. He has also conceptualized and is actively working on the implementation of 'Financial Literacy for All', an initiative aimed at providing financial education free of cost to a billion Indians.

FINANCIAL AFFAIRS OF THE COMMON MAN

Master the Art of Personal Finance Management

ANIL LAMBA

PENGUIN
BUSINESS

An imprint of Penguin Random House

PENGUIN BUSINESS

USA | Canada | UK | Ireland | Australia
New Zealand | India | South Africa | China | Singapore

Penguin Business is part of the Penguin Random House group of companies whose addresses can be found at global.penguinrandomhouse.com

Published by Penguin Random House India Pvt. Ltd
4th Floor, Capital Tower 1, MG Road,
Gurugram 122 002, Haryana, India

Penguin Random House India

First published in Portfolio by Penguin Random House India 2019
Published in Penguin Business 2022

Copyright © Anil Lamba 2019

All rights reserved

10 9 8 7 6 5 4 3 2

The views and opinions expressed in this book are the author's own and the facts are as reported by him which have been verified to the extent possible, and the publishers are not in any way liable for the same.

ISBN 9780143457459

For sale in the Indian Subcontinent only

Typeset in Myriad Pro

Printed at Manipal Technologies Limited, India

This book is sold subject to the condition that it shall not, by way of trade or otherwise, be lent, resold, hired out, or otherwise circulated without the publisher's prior consent in any form of binding or cover other than that in which it is published and without a similar condition including this condition being imposed on the subsequent purchaser.

www.penguin.co.in

FSC www.fsc.org MIX Paper | Supporting responsible forestry FSC® C043100

This is a legitimate digitally printed version of the book and therefore might not have certain extra finishing on the cover.

To my countrymen.

I reassert my commitment to devote a higher percentage of my time each successive year to spreading financial literacy among those who cannot afford to acquire it, in a bid towards creating a financially intelligent India.

Acknowledgements

This book would not have been written had my editor, Lohit Jagwani, not asked me to do so. I am thankful to him for not only making the suggestion, but also thereafter being a pillar of support at every stage. He would ever so gently remind me when deadlines loomed, prod me into action when he thought I was being lazy and keep tabs with clockwork regularity to monitor the progress being made. Thank you, Lohit, for bearing with my erratic schedules and for indulging my interference in every aspect of the book's production and design.

I am fortunate to have in my daughter, Mehek, an in-house editor. She painstakingly went through every word of the book based on a subject which I know is not her favourite by a long shot. With her eye for detail and proficiency in the language, she ensured that not only was the phraseology appropriate and the grammar correct, but that the full stops, commas and semicolons were also in place. Thank you, Mehek. I am blessed to have you in my life.

If any errors have still managed to creep in, it would be the result of tinkering on my part post the editing done by both Lohit and Mehek.

Writing a book requires one to sit for long hours, reading, researching, brooding and typing in turns. It also tends to make a person quite antisocial and a recluse, the brunt of which is borne by the wife. Thank you, Nicky, my partner for life, for being my pillar of support as always and encouraging me in all of my endeavours.

Learning is a lifelong pursuit. One can learn as much from books as by observing the actions of those whose success can be attributed to intelligent financial decision-making. It gives me great pleasure when I see my teenaged son, Vedant, at a very early age, handling money and taking business decisions with aplomb. From him, there is much to learn.

And lastly, grateful thanks to my mother-in-law who continues to shower her blessings on all of us, and Praphulla and Digambar, my right and left hand at Lamcon, for their constant support.

Preface

For a nation to achieve sustained growth and prosperity, it is essential that its people be financially intelligent.

It is an acknowledged fact that the single most important cause of business failures worldwide is financial mismanagement.

But this is equally true of individuals and families too. Else how is it that certain families with relatively lesser incomes appear to manage their expenses quite comfortably while others, having substantially higher earnings, are either perpetually running short of cash or always seem to be in debt?

It is not only in the interest of the economic health of a nation that financial literacy is important but also for the level of satisfaction and overall productivity of its population.

Those who cannot manage money are constantly running behind on monthly expenses and loan instalments, and find it difficult to make ends meet. They are also less satisfied with their life experiences. And this results in a lower happiness quotient, which eventually reflects in lower productivity and inferior quality of whatever they do, make or grow, and the vicious cycle becomes self-perpetuating.

The solution to many of mankind's problems lies in its ability to manage money.

If there is going to be one stumbling block in this nation's growth story it will be financial illiteracy, a deficiency of financial acumen, among its people.

Your success in life, to a large extent, depends on your level of financial intelligence.

I have often wondered what, in the last couple of decades, has led to India becoming a more prosperous nation, an upcoming superpower and an acknowledged leader of the Asian subcontinent.

We have the same problems as before. We still have a burgeoning population and an alarmingly high level of corruption. Our bureaucrats still possess the same feudal mindset. Our cleanliness and hygiene standards, infrastructure, pollution levels etc., are still a far cry from what is desired.

Then what has brought about this drastically transformed image of India among the global community? What is responsible for the enviable rate of its Gross Domestic Product (GDP) growth? Why is it that India was, by and large, unaffected, even as much of the world went into a tailspin, post the sub-prime crisis?
The more I think about it the more convinced I get that the reason for this transformation in India is that ever since Manmohan Singh and P. V. Narasimha Rao initiated the economic reforms process in 1991, India's finance management has been handled by people who understand finance management.

If you improve finance management in nations, they prosper. If you improve finance management in corporations, they flourish. If you improve finance management among individuals and families, they become financially secure, happier and more productive.

Effective personal finance management is necessary not only to enable individuals to lead comfortable lives, meet all financial responsibilities, educate their children and to eat and live well, but also to provide for the time when the income stops.

One should strive to see that post-retirement the standard of one's living does not drop. In fact it should ideally enhance because one has more time available to be spent pursuing hobbies and travelling the world.

All this will be possible if we learn how to manage money.

The problem is that most of us either don't understand it or do not have the time to do so.

We are completely engrossed in trying to generate more income (and there is nothing wrong with that). But what has already been earned lies untended and unmanaged.

My conviction is that no matter at what stage you are in life, stop doing whatever you do in your full-time occupation and start spending maybe a quarter of that time managing the money you have already made. You will probably earn as much as, if not more than, what you do now.

This book is an attempt to give you the knowledge, the tools and the information required to be able to take charge of your personal finance management.

Contents

Chapter 01

Investment Options

The best advice that can be given in the matter of personal finance is to start investing early.

Investment is putting money in certain income-generating assets.

Various avenues of investment are available to an investor and it can often be a difficult task to ensure that the money is invested in the most appropriate or the most profitable combination of assets.

One is faced with conflicting options. Should one invest in long-term or short-term assets, high-returns-high-risk or low-return-but-relatively-safer investment, in real estate or in shares, debentures or fixed deposits?

Each category of investment has its own attractions and disadvantages. The poor investor is often at a loss as to what should be chosen.

However, no right-thinking person should undermine the need for planning in investment.

The investment portfolio of an individual, to a large extent, depends on one's appetite for risk.

Those who are more risk-averse would prefer to invest in fixed deposits, post office schemes and government bonds. Those not so averse to it would delve into equities.

There are others who will choose the middle path and opt for investing in mutual funds while the adventurous will indulge in trading in derivatives, commodities and even currency.

Not to forget, the particular fascination Indians have for buying gold.

Additionally, it is everybody's dream to own a house and invest in real estate.

Depending on one's tax bracket and tax liability, one could also invest in instruments that are eligible for a tax rebate.

Risk vs Return

Most people are aware of the directly proportional risk-return correlation—the higher the risk the better the return and vice versa. This equation is often a cause for dilemma among many investors. The greed instinct attracts us towards investments that have the potential to generate higher returns while prudence demands the preservation of one's hard-earned money.

It is important to decide at the very outset what you expect from your investments. J. Kenfield Morley[1] said that 'In investing money, the amount of interest that you want depends on whether you want to eat well or sleep well.'

Inflation

One needs to understand how harmful the effect of inflation can be, particularly for a retired person. It is a state all salaried employees will be in one day.

Normally, inflation should encourage expenditure and deter saving. After all, one can get much more worth and value from money spent now than a few years later. This is exactly what happens in some of the affluent countries like the USA, where the saving rates are quite low.

But then this is possible in countries with low levels of unemployment and social security payment in case of unemployment. Without these, as in the case of India, it becomes necessary to save for a rainy day and for old age.

The three parameters

While planning an investment of any type the three major parameters that one needs to consider are **safety, liquidity** and **return on investment**. There is another aspect—life insurance—which though important does not strictly fall in the category of savings and investment. This is catered for by the insurance policies and the unit-linked insurance plans (ULIPs) offered by various companies.

While subjective preference between liquidity and rate of return may vary from person to person, most individuals would rate security of capital (certainty of return at the end of the contracted duration) as the highest priority.

While planning an investment of any type the three major parameters that one needs to consider are those of safety, liquidity and return on investment.

From a security perspective the total savings instruments can be grouped into:

1. those supported by the government, like public-sector banks, postal deposits, the Unit Trust of India etc., and,
2. those offered by the corporate sector, like fixed deposits with private and public corporations, investment in private mutual funds, debentures issued by companies and equity shares of private-sector companies.

Safety

As far as safety of capital is concerned, the government-based investments are obviously the more secure ones, with very little to choose between them.

With respect to investments with the corporate sector, fixed deposits with public-sector companies would be relatively safer. These are followed by debentures, which are long-term securities yielding a fixed rate of interest.

Other instruments are fixed deposits with private-sector companies and investments in equity shares.

Equity shares rank last in safety as the value of one's investment is prone to fluctuation, depending on the forces of demand and supply.

This should not make one feel that all equity shares are extremely risky. There are many blue-chip companies which have maintained a very steady growth rate and where (barring speculative effects over a short duration) the value of the shares has always continued to show a rise.

Liquidity

This is an important parameter to measure the efficacy of a good investment.

The most liquid investment would, of course, be a current account (opened by businesses) in a bank which fetches no interest.

The next would possibly be savings deposit accounts in banks and with post offices.

Next in the sequence would come units of mutual funds.

Equity shares would be extremely liquid unless the company in which one holds stock is in trouble and there is very little trading going on in the company's scrip in the stock market.

Gold, silver and bullion are also easy to liquidate.

Next on the liquidity scale would be the debentures for which purchasers are not readily available.

Still lower down in respect of liquidity would possibly be fixed deposits with companies which can neither be transferred nor encashed. These fixed deposit receipts cannot even be used as collaterals to raise loans from banks.

Fixed deposits in banks would however show up better in the light of liquidity, since banks permit you loans/overdraft facilities at a nominal interest above that paid on deposits.

At the bottom of the scale would be real estate assets which usually cannot be liquidated on demand.

Returns on investment

The return on investment is available to an investor in the form of periodical returns (monthly, quarterly, six-monthly or yearly) and in the form of capital appreciation (relevant mainly to equity shares and debentures). There are special income tax concessions for long-term capital gains. The returns on investment are closely linked with security and liquidity. The higher the security and liquidity the lower the rate of return and vice versa.

Options abound

So where should one invest?
What should an ideal investment portfolio comprise?

Liquid assets

You must keep a small amount of money in fairly liquid interest-bearing assets (short-term and risk-free) or deposit a certain amount in a public provident fund (PPF) account (relatively long-term but risk-free).

This would be necessary in case of an emergency where funds are needed urgently. It would be possible to immediately withdraw the amount or to take a loan against the balance in the account.

Equity and real estate

For long-term investment, building an equity portfolio or investing in real estate may be a good idea. While the former is accompanied by high risk, the latter is a safe, low-risk option.

Equity

When investing in equity, you would do well to find a good broker who will not only buy and sell on your behalf but will also be a source of sound advice on where and when to invest.

This has perhaps been the highest money-making avenue over the years. What was once considered to be an activity indulged in by only a few has now become commonplace.

The biggest advantage of investing in shares is that not only does your capital grow, but you also stand to earn money through dividends, while at the same time contributing to nation-building through provision of capital to deserving entrepreneurs.

Property

During the early stages of your career, it is understandable that one may not have large investible surpluses and hence acquiring real estate may not be possible. However, this is one investment that you should make as soon as you can afford to make the down payment and pay the equal monthly instalments (EMIs).

For one thing, land or building assets in the long-run always appreciate.

And property also holds the potential of generating further regular income if it is let-out.

There are, of course, those who have made their fortunes through just trading in property.

After all, it is not called **real estate** for nothing.

Gold

There's an irrational magic associated with this otherwise useless yellow metal. Over the centuries, gold has been a measure of wealth and prosperity.

In India, the craze to acquire this metal, which is almost a dead investment, borders on obsession. This is so since most investors in gold do not buy it in raw or 'demat' form but do so in the form of jewellery. No matter how much the price of gold appreciates, such persons will never sell their ornaments. Selling of gold is the last resort reserved for those in dire straits.

It is this that makes investing in gold a losing proposition.

You must have observed the extreme variability in the characteristics of the available investments in the market.

There is also a vast variation in the investors in term of age, tax brackets, vocations and personal preferences.

These two aspects put together give rise to an infinite combination of investment instruments to suit the objective and subjective tastes of the investor adding, in the process, considerable difficulty in the problems of choice.

To make matters worse, many individuals do not have the time to keep themselves updated regarding the different investment opportunities available.

The complexity of investment instruments coupled with the lack of time available with busy executives and business persons has given rise to a new breed of consultants called investment advisers.

This job was earlier performed by investment brokers. Over time people felt that it was a specialized function not quite within the competence of an average broker whose advice could often be coloured by brokerage considerations.

1. C Foster Stanback, *The Book of Financial Wisdom*, Lulu, 2010.

‘Beware of little expenses: a small leak can sink a great ship.’

Benjamin Franklin

Chapter 02

Effect of Inflation on Investments

What is inflation?

Inflation is a phenomenon of rising prices or falling purchasing powers.

Price, as you may well be aware, is a function of demand and supply.

Consider an example:

Let's say one group of people—Group A—is engaged in the manufacture of cars and another group—Group B—is in the need of cars.

The capacity of Group A is to make 100 cars and the requirement of Group B is for 100 cars.

If a car sells for 500,000, chances are it will continue to sell at that price.

Now imagine one person gets added to Group B and their requirement of cars goes up to 101. The capacity of Group A to manufacture cars is still 100. What do you think will happen to the price of cars? It will go up.

When the demand for a product or commodity goes up, its price goes up.

What if one person gets added to Group A, and they now make 101 cars. But the requirement of cars of Group B is still 100. What will happen to the price? It will fall.

When the supply of a product or commodity goes up, its price comes down.

Each time demand goes up, will price go up? Each time that supply increases, will price fall?

Not necessarily.

In the above case, when Group B's requirement for cars went up to 101, what if Group A had responded by making 101 cars? The price would not have gone up.

So, the maxim gets modified slightly:

When the demand for a product or commodity goes up, its price goes up, unless supply responds.

When Group A manufactures 101 cars and Group B is willing to purchase 101 cars, the price will not fall.

When the supply for a product or commodity goes up, its price will fall, unless demand responds.

In order for price to rise or fall it is necessary that there is unilateral increase either in demand or supply.

What causes inflation?

This creation of money to meet expenditure is called deficit financing. One of the fallouts of deficit financing is inflation.

It often happens that governments of nations find the expected receipts of the year (from taxes and other forms of earnings and borrowings) to be lesser than the expected expenditures (on payment of salaries for running the government, payment of interest on loans and funding development projects).

When the earnings plus borrowings are not sufficient to meet expenditures, they then resort to printing or creation of money.

This creation of money to meet expenditure is called **deficit financing.**

One of the fallouts of deficit financing is inflation.

Why is deficit financing inflationary?

For a moment, imagine each person in the country earns an amount equal to 'x' per month.

In the following year everybody works twice as hard and starts earning '2x' per month.

The spending power of the entire population has gone up.

The buying power of the nation has doubled. Will it lead to price rise?

The answer is no!

Why not?

How did the buying power double?

It is because everyone worked twice as hard.

Which means they must have also produced twice as much.

While on the one hand the buying power has doubled, on the other hand the supply of goods and services has also doubled.

It is non-inflationary.

But when governments print money to spend, there is merely an increase in the supply of money without a corresponding increase in the supply of goods and services. More money now chases the same quantity of goods and services, and this leads to inflation.

When governments print money to spend, there is merely an increase in the supply of money without a corresponding increase in the supply of goods and services. More money now chases the same quantity of goods and services, and this leads to inflation.

Get off the treadmill

The effect of inflation is bad enough even when you are younger, since you need to make sure that your rate of growth of earnings outpaces the rate of inflation. Else it will appear that you are making more money than before, whereas in real terms the purchasing power of your income will actually be falling.

While you are still working, the impact of inflation is partially, or entirely, offset by a continuous increase in income or profit. In the case of government and public-sector employees and pensioners, this gets done by payment of dearness allowance (DA) which is a cost of living adjustment allowance. The amount to be paid is calculated as a percentage of the employees' basic salary to mitigate the impact of inflation on people.

But inflation is a killer once you have stopped earning. If you have not invested wisely, it might well happen that the nest egg you kept aside to live on post-retirement may not even suffice for six months.

The purchasing power of your savings dwindles as goods and services increase in price.

How much will you need to compensate for the impact of inflation?

Unfortunately, it is not possible to predict inflation with any precision.

Of course, past data can give an indication but there is no guarantee that the trend will not change.

The rule of 72

Are you aware of the rule of 72?

If you wish to understand how long it will take for your money to double, divide 72 by the rate of interest. You can get a rough estimate of how many years it will take for the initial investment to duplicate itself.

If your money is growing at the rate of 6 per cent, then divide 72 by 6. In twelve years, the amount will double.

If the rate of interest is 8 per cent, 72/8 = 9. The money will double in nine years. And so on.

So, if the expected rate of inflation is say 6 per cent

(consistently year on year), 72/6 = 12. Every twelve years the prices would have doubled (or the purchasing power of money would become half in twelve years).
What costs 100 today, will cost 200 after twelve years, 400 after twenty-four years, and 800 after thirty-six years.

Which means that if you are twenty-four years old today, and plan to retire at the age of sixty (thirty-six years later), you will need to earn eight times the amount you are earning today to maintain your existing standard of living.

Assuming a life expectancy of say eighty-five years, the amount required closer to age eighty-five would be sixty-four times your current earnings.

This calculation is based on maintaining your existing standards. But as your standard of living would be rising year after year, you would ideally expect the levels of comfort that you were enjoying at the time of retirement. So, the amount required would be even higher.

The rule of 72 does not give exact calculations but an approximation. The numbers cited above are therefore not accurate, but nevertheless serve the purpose of communicating the toll that inflation can take on your purchasing power and the need to take steps to counter it to be able to live comfortably after retirement.

What can be done?

What steps can you take to ensure that your retirement savings will take care of all your needs, despite the threat of inflation?

Your investments and the value of your assets need to increase in value beyond inflation levels so that you have the amount necessary to afford the products and services needed once you become a senior citizen.

You are planning for the unknown since inflation is a moving target that really cannot be predicted.

> **Inflation does not reduce the amount of money you have saved up. In fact, that amount may well be increasing due to interest earned. But it does reduce the buying power of that money.**

In order to protect your interests and your family's well-being, you need to plan now to ensure the value of your investments stays ahead of inflation.

Inflation does not reduce the amount of money you have saved up. In fact, that amount may well be increasing due to interest earned. But it does reduce the buying power of that money.

With increasing costs of living, your ability to buy becomes lesser and lesser using the money available today.

Remember, a few years ago watching a movie cost maybe a fifth of what it does today.

If your money lies invested in a savings or even a fixed deposit account in a bank, the interest rate it is earning is probably a lot less than the rate of inflation. This means that the cost of goods and services is rising much faster than the interest you might be earning.

So what must you do?

You must incorporate inflation into your planning.

It will be naive on your part to assume that the amount you have saved up today will be enough to last you in the years to come.

Out of your concern for safety, you may have invested in bonds, money market funds and bank savings accounts. But these investments may not provide enough growth to outpace inflation.

You will have to move out of your comfort zone and invest in stocks and other instruments in order to add a level of growth to your portfolio that can keep you ahead of inflation.

Inflation is a fact of life. You, in your personal capacity, cannot do anything about it. You can only attempt to arrange your affairs to manage it.

'Money is like love; it kills slowly and painfully the one who withholds it, and enlivens the other who turns it on his fellow man.'

Kahlil Gibran

Chapter 03

The Power of Compounding

What is compound interest?

If you make a fixed deposit of Rs 100 and earn interest at the rate of 10 per cent per annum, in Year 1 you will earn Rs 10.

If you withdraw the interest for your personal need keeping the principal intact, the following year you will again earn the same Rs 10.

If you withdraw the interest once again, the third year too you will earn Rs 10.

This is simple interest.

But if you don't withdraw the interest amount in Year 1 and leave it in the bank, the closing balance in your account at the end of Year 1 will be Rs 110.

The following year you will earn interest at the rate of 10 per cent on Rs 110, that is you will earn Rs 11.

If again the interest remains in your account, the balance would have increased to Rs 121 and you will earn Rs 12.1 as interest.

When you earn interest not only on the principal sum but also on the interest earned, it is called compound interest.

If you had kept your money in the bank for ten years and were earning a simple interest of 10 per cent, at the end of the period you would have earned an interest of Rs 100.

But if you were reinvesting the interest earned and earning compound interest, the interest earned would have been Rs 160.

The difference in interest earned, though substantial, may still not appear to be very impressive. But the benefit of compounding really comes to the fore over the long term. Compounding can be done on a monthly, quarterly, half-yearly or an annual basis.

If the interest is calculated on an annual basis and added to the bank balance, it is called annual compounding.

In case of monthly compounding, each month the interest for the month is added to the account and the following month you earn interest on the principal plus the monthly interest.

Let us see the impact of compounding over an extended period of time.

Earnings			
Amount Invested = 10000	Simple Interest	Yearly Compounding	Monthly Compounding
Year 1	1000	1000	1047
Year 10	10,000	16,000	17,000
Year 25	25,000	98,300	1,10,500
Year 40	40,000	4,42,600	5,27,000
Year 50	50,000	11,63,900	14,43,700
Year 60	60,000	30,34,800	39,25,200

It is often said that a person no less than Albert Einstein had called compound interest the most powerful force in the universe. Whether he did say so or not, there is no doubt about the power of compound interest.

There is a story I had read about a king who played a game of chess with a simple farmer.

At the end of a closely fought game the king lost.

Pleased with the farmer's effort, the king wanted to reward him and asked the farmer what he wanted.

The farmer said, 'Just give me one grain of wheat for the first square of chess, and double it for each square thereafter.' (Which meant one grain for the first square, two for the second, four for the third, eight for the fourth and so on, for the sixty-four squares on the board.)

The king readily agreed and the farmer's wish was granted. When the total calculation was made it worked out to 18,446,744,073,709,551,615 grains of wheat or over 700,000 million tonnes of wheat.

No wonder the power of compounding has been called the eighth wonder of the world. One who understands it, earns it and the one who does not, pays it.

The farmer understood it and the king paid it.

No wonder the power of compounding has been called the eighth wonder of the world. One who understands it, earns it and the one who does not, pays it.

How can you benefit from the power of compounding?

You can make compounding work for you by:

1. Beginning the saving habit as early as possible and,
2. Saving regularly.

If the power of compound interest is understood at a young age, the youth would have a great incentive for starting to save early. Those who grasp the implications enjoy huge financial benefits.

The sooner one learns about compound interest, the bigger the financial difference it can make.

The problem is that for the first few years compounding does not appear very impressive. It's when compounding periods reach fifteen to thirty years that the amount really starts to add up.

Compounding gives the maximum benefit when you let your savings or investment grow over a longer time horizon.

The earlier you start, the longer compounding can work for your money.

Take a look at this example illustrating the advantage of saving early:

Karan starts investing Rs 1000 per month at the age of forty and earns an annual rate of interest of 8 per cent. At the age of sixty-five he would have accumulated Rs 9,57,367 (on his total investment of Rs 3,00,000 over a period of twenty-five years).

Rita begins investing Rs 1000 per month at the age of twenty-five, earning 8 per cent per annum and deposits for only fifteen years till the age of forty. She would have a balance of Rs 25,57,000 in her account at the age of sixty-five (on her total investment of Rs 1,80,000)

Karan has invested for twenty-five years and Rita has merely put aside the money for fifteen years. And yet at the age of retirement the money available with Rita is almost three times of what Karan has.

I would encourage all youngsters reading this book to start the habit of saving from tomorrow itself.

And I will urge parents of young children to invest some money in the children's account soon after the kids are born. If you do that, the child can have a saving horizon of about sixty years. You could deposit money till the child starts earning, and thereafter the child starts depositing in an account that is already about eighteen to twenty years old.

Such kids, by the time they reach retirement, may just find that this account alone can sustain them for the rest of their lives.

'Money is a terrible master but an excellent servant.'

P.T. Barnum

Chapter 04

Importance of Insurance

A. Life Insurance

In this chapter let us discuss the need and importance of both

1. **Life insurance**
2. **Medical insurance**

What is the rationale behind having a life insurance policy?

It is that if something happens to the breadwinner of the family, the person should not be missed at least insofar as the financial contributions of the person to meet the family's expenditure are concerned.

An estimate should be made of the kind of income stream the family must continue to receive even if the income provider is no more.

For argument's sake let's say that amount is Rs 10,000 per month.

One must now work out the amount that should be left behind, in case one day the person is no more, to enable the family to continue to receive that income stream.

Let's say that sum is Rs 1,000,000.

Who is more in need of insurance? A relatively richer person or the one who is poorer?

It is the latter.

If one has already accumulated assets of that value, one does not need insurance.

But if one does not own property worth Rs 1 million, it is possible to have an insurance policy for that amount by paying a fraction of that sum as premium.

As one accumulates assets in other forms, the need for insurance progressively reduces.

The poorer a person is, the greater the need for insurance.

Paradoxically it is the rich that are usually insured while the poor most often are not.

It is so important to be correctly insured. Most people are either under insured or wrongly insured.

The poorer a person is, the greater the need for insurance. Paradoxically it is the rich that are usually insured while the poor most often are not.

There are only three policies worth talking about when it comes to life insurance:

1. A whole life policy
2. An endowment policy and
3. A term policy

A **whole life policy** is one where the sum assured is never received by the person insured. When the person is no more the insurance money goes to the beneficiary.

In case of most whole life insurance plans, the amount and duration of premium payments are the same for as long as the insured is alive. But some whole life policies allow the premiums to be paid in a single instalment, or for shorter periods, or until the age of sixty-five.

An **endowment policy** is a life insurance policy where a lump sum is paid on maturity of the policy or on death. Typical maturities are at ten, fifteen or twenty years, up to a certain age limit.

Term life insurance policies provide pure insurance coverage at the lowest cost. There is no maturity amount to be paid in case the insured person survives the term of the policy. It is similar to vehicle insurance where, in case the vehicle meets with an accident, one can claim the amount of damages from the insurance company..And in case no accident takes place the premium is written off.

Since, in the case of both the endowment and whole life insurance plans, the premium paid along with a certain amount of interest and bonus is returned to either the policyholder or the beneficiaries, these are considered to be savings plans that build cash value.

Endowments have a shorter coverage period and mature sooner, usually in ten to twenty years. Whole life policies are designed to last for the entire life of the insured, so these policies mature when the insured policyholder reaches the age of ninety-five or 100.

The **term plan**, on the other hand, is a pure expense since nothing is returned if the insured person survives the term.

Endowments plans are the most expensive, having higher monthly premiums—the shorter the endowment term, the higher the premiums.

Whole life policies have relatively lower premiums. Term policies work out the cheapest.

Whole life and endowment premiums are higher than term life insurance premiums since only a part of the premium goes towards insurance and the balance is invested for future returns, to be paid upon maturity.

This makes term policies the most attractive since one can take policies with substantially high coverage at affordable prices.

Never combine insurance and investment

Most people take insurance for the wrong reasons, such as to reduce the income tax liability (since premiums enjoy a deduction from taxable income), as an investment, or a combination of the two.

Insurance has an important role to play in personal finance management. It is to protect one's family from financial difficulty. Often a person takes a loan to purchase property. If, before the property has been acquired, the person happens to die, the family is neither in a position to pay the balance amount due toward the property nor pay back the debt. In such situations, if the person was insured, the money received from the insurance company can save the day.

But when insurance is perceived as an investment, one gets tempted to take the wrong type of policy.

There is a plan called the 'money-back', where a certain portion of the sum assured is paid back to the policyholder, say, every five years.
It is one of the most popular plans sold by insurance companies.

> **Life insurance policies are taken for the benefit of the beneficiaries and not the person insured. The moment you plan to get the money back in your own lifetime you have defeated the objective of taking life insurance.**

The insurance agent makes it sound so attractive that most people opt for it. It is one, however, of the worst policies to take.

Life insurance policies are taken for the benefit of the beneficiaries and not the person insured. The moment you plan to get the money back in your own lifetime you have defeated the objective of taking life insurance.

Besides, I don't know of a worse investment than life insurance.

What makes life insurance attractive is the package—the insurance coverage plus a mediocre investment.

However, if you keep the two separate—have a pure insurance and a pure investment—you will get the best of both, an appropriate insurance coverage as well as an excellent investment, and may still have money to spare.

Instead of buying a money-back plan for a certain coverage, if you choose a term plan of the same value (or even a whole life policy of the same sum assured), you would have an equally good insurance at a far cheaper premium. If you invest the leftover money anywhere else, you will probably earn more on that sum than you would have on the entire amount paid as premium for a money back plan.

Alternately, if you have earmarked a certain amount that you would like to pay as premium per annum, the sum assured that you will get if you opt for a whole life or a term plan would be substantially higher than what you will get from a money-back policy.

But the insurance agents will typically push for plans like money-back, not because these are better policies but because they get higher commissions by selling them.

You need to have the understanding to choose the most appropriate insurance policy to suit your requirements.

B. Medical Insurance

In addition to having an adequate life insurance policy, which is to take care of the family's financial needs after one's passing away, it is equally important to have the right health insurance. This is to ensure that all the medical expenses of oneself and the family can be taken care of during one's lifetime. Medical problems can take place without any prior intimation or warning and can potentially drain away one's entire life's savings, and still fall short. A small amount of money, paid towards medical premium, can help avoid financial trauma at the time of a medical emergency. A very important aspect of personal finance planning, therefore, is to arrange for suitable health insurance.

To secure the well-being of your family members and protect your savings while getting their medical treatments done from quality hospitals, choosing an appropriate family health cover plan is a wise decision. This sort of a comprehensive plan offers complete protection for each member of the family and can help you lead a happier and healthier life free from all tensions.

As medical care advances and treatments improve, health care costs also increase. One is more likely to get routine and preventive care if one has health insurance. People with health insurance are more likely to have a regular doctor and to get care when they need it.

Today, it is heartening to note that more and more people are opting for health insurance, even though we still have a long way to go. Large segments of our population are not so covered, particularly the poorer segments. And even if government schemes may exist, its awareness does not. It is important to educate the masses about the need for medical insurance and the existence of free and / or affordable policies which are within the means of the poorest members of the community.

For those who can afford to buy health insurance, the first step towards such a purchase is to understand and estimate your requirements. What is an adequate health cover plan is one of the most vital questions that needs to be answered.

You may need a plan for yourself as an individual or you might be looking for a complete family health coverage plan.

In either case, you will need to know the cost, terms and conditions, and services offered.

The easiest way to go about it would be to request for a free quote on the website of the insurance company of your choice. All the major players of the insurance sector have their presence on this platform providing complete, trustworthy and valuable suggestions through online insurance.

If you are a salaried individual, then it is likely that your organization may provide health insurance protection to its employees. This is also a very good way to insure your health treatment costs. Of course, an employee can get additional cover, in case there is an upper limit to the amount that the employer provides.

Best time to buy a health insurance policy:

It is obvious that you should not wait until you or a family member becomes seriously ill to try to purchase health insurance. The right time to buy a health insurance policy is NOW. Medical costs will only escalate in the future owing to overall inflation and the rise in the cost of living, besides other factors. The sooner the realization of this truth sets in the better it is.

It is best to buy a health insurance policy at a young age to avail the many benefits.

Why should one get health insurance at a young age?

There are many reasons why opting for a health insurance policy at a young age is advisable. Most of these advantages serve to reduce the upfront and effective cost of the policy.

The premium charged on medical policies depends on the insured person's age at the time of taking the policy. If one opts for a policy at a young age, one can avail of a lower premium.

Many health plans offer wide coverage, the costs of which only increase as one grows older and owing to more medical complications. Taking a health insurance policy at a young age ensures that you have greater coverage.

Buying a health insurance policy in your late forties will only increase your financial burden with reduced benefits. Many health insurance providers exclude many pre-existing conditions from getting covered which defeats the purpose of opting for a health insurance policy.

Besides, health insurance premiums enjoy a tax rebate. Buying a health insurance policy at a young age allows one to enjoy tax benefits for a longer period, which also effectively reduces the out-of-pocket cost of the premium.

Most insurance companies offer a 'no-claims bonus' in the absence of any claims in the preceding year of a policy term. If you buy a health insurance policy at a young age, you can avail a cumulative bonus as you will most likely renew your policy every year. As a result, the bonus accumulated increases your coverage amount which will prove to be an advantage at later stages of life when you are old and grey. No-claims bonuses may range from 5 per cent to 100 per cent of the sum insured in most cases.

Most health insurance policies prescribe a waiting period of one to three months during which claims cannot be made, even if there is a medical emergency. Buying a health insurance policy at a young age, when one is in robust health, is advantageous as, barring a misfortune, the waiting period can be passed without any concern.

It also makes for good financial planning since buying a health insurance policy at a young age not only gives greater coverage but also helps in planning one's finances in a better way. When one has adequate medical cover to take care of any health emergencies, one can focus better on making other long-term investments.

Things to take care of while buying health insurance

Ensure that you purchase a comprehensive mediclaim policy which provides sufficient coverage against future medical expenses.

The medical policy should not only cover hospitalization, but also pre- and post-hospitalization expenses.

Besides this, the plan chosen should offer coverage for out patient department (OPD) check-ups, dental treatment as well as maternity and critical illness coverage. To provide for serious illnesses like cancer or heart attack, the feature of lifelong renewal can be helpful.

'Never spend your money before you have earned it.'

Thomas Jefferson

Chapter 05

Understanding Financial Statements

A very useful habit you must cultivate is to prepare a personal balance sheet. It will give you immense clarity about your own finances, the investments made and assets purchased, and will help improve your control over money management.

Let us first understand these two very important financial statements—the profit and loss account (P&L) and the balance sheet—from a business perspective. I will then tell you how to use the understanding to make personal balance sheets.

A balance sheet and a P&L account are two financial statements prepared by every business organization.

The P&L account reveals incomes and expenses and a balance sheet lists out an organization's assets and liabilities.

Profit and loss account

As its name suggests, this statement is prepared to find out whether an organization has made a profit or a loss.

The P&L account lists out **incomes** on one side and **expenses** on the other.

When incomes exceed expenses, the organization makes a profit. When expenses are greater than incomes, it makes a loss.

Some examples of expenses are:

1. purchase of raw materials,
2. salaries and wages paid to workers and staff,
3. travelling expenses,
4. various kinds of selling and administrative expenses,
5. interest on money borrowed.

The principal source of income for a business, that is, the income generated by carrying out its core activities, is shown as sales.

Income generated through non-core activities appears as 'other income'.

Profit and Loss Account	
Expenses	**Income**
Materials	Sales ← *Top Line*
Wages and Salaries	Other Income
Selling Expenses	
Admin Expenses	
Interest	
Profit ← *Bottom Line*	

For a healthy organization, the bulk of its income should come from sales, that is, its core operations. If a large part of the income comes from non-core activities, it is a cause of worry.

Sales, which appears on the top of the P&L account on the right-hand side, is referred to as the top line in financial jargon, and the figure of profit, appearing at the bottom on the left-hand side, is called the bottom line.

Balance sheet

The two sides of the balance sheet reveal liabilities and assets.

Balance Sheet	
Liabilities	**Assets**
Capital	**Fixed Assets** Land, Building, Plant, Machinery
Loan	
Current Liabilities Creditors, Bank Overdraft	**Current Assets** Debtors, Bank Balance, Inventory

Liabilities represent what you owe.

Businesses borrow money from the owners as well as from outsiders.

Borrowings from owners is called **capital**. What is borrowed from outsiders is classified as **loans**.

Both the owners' as well as the lenders' contributions are reflected on the liabilities' side of the balance sheet.

Besides, there may be liabilities toward suppliers and vendors for materials and services purchased. These appear as current liabilities.

Assets represent what you own, or the things that you have purchased by spending the money that you have borrowed.

Typical assets include investments in land, buildings, machinery, vehicles, computers, tools, etc. These appear on a balance sheet as fixed assets.

The second category of assets is called current assets, which includes items like inventory of materials, cash and bank balances and debts.

Evaluating the financial health by understanding and reading its balance sheet is an essential skill for all persons.

But is it also necessary for them to know how to make these statements?

In an organization it is the responsibility of the accountants to prepare financial statements. However, all who are in charge of running and managing the business must know how to read these statements.

A common misconception is that in order to learn how to read balance sheets one must also know how to make them. This is not true at all. It is quite possible to learn to read, interpret and understand balance sheets without knowing how they are made.

It is quite possible to learn to read, interpret and understand balance sheets without knowing how they are made.

While everyone who is expected to read a balance sheet need not know how to prepare one, it's really not as difficult as many fear it might be. In fact, I can actually teach you how to make one in about three minutes.

The normal perception is that it takes several years to learn the art and science of bookkeeping and the making of financial statements. That is in fact true if you learn in the conventional way.

But what I am going to teach you is not the conventional method. I'm going to show you a far shorter way in which we will eliminate the bookkeeping and directly prepare these statements using an extremely simple common-sense technique.

What you must understand is that whatever happens in an organization is either an expense, income, liability, or asset.

All financial transactions that take place get recorded in a set of books collectively called 'accounts.'

Accounts get summarized periodically and the result is presented in the form of two financial statements—a P&L account and a balance sheet.

Which means these two statements reflect a summarized picture of everything that has happened in an organization over a certain period.

And, between them, the P&L account and the balance sheet reveal incomes and expenses, and liabilities and assets.

This tells you that nothing can happen in any organization which will not eventually result in one out of these four.

So, if you wish to learn how to make these statements, look at each transaction as it takes place, try and figure out which of the four it is and directly transfer it to these statements, bypassing the entire accounting process.

It is not that easy, it is even easier.

Actually, there are only two types of transactions that take place—those that bring money in and those that take money away.

Expenses and assets involve spending and incomes and liabilities represent receipts.

If you spend money on the purchase of a car it will be shown as an asset and when you fill fuel it will be an expense.

Similarly, if you sell goods or services and in exchange receive money, it is an income, and if you receive money by way of a loan it is a liability.

You now realize that you don't have to choose out of four but out of two options.

When money comes in, you need to choose between income and liability and when it goes out the choice is between expense and asset. Record the item in the relevant quadrant and your P&L account and balance sheet are ready.

'Both poverty and riches are the offspring of thought.'

Napoleon Hill

Chapter 06

Make Your Personal Balance Sheet

Make it a habit to prepare your personal balance sheet

Now that you have understood how these statements are made, I would strongly recommend that each of you get into the habit of preparing your personal balance sheets. It will give you immense clarity about your own finances.

Let me show you how to go about it.

Step 1: Prepare an opening balance sheet

To do that I suggest you make a note of all the assets that you own, for example, house, car, furniture, television set, refrigerator, bank balance, investments in shares and mutual funds, jewellery, etc. (all of these must be at the cost at which acquired).

Show these on the assets' side of your balance sheet.

Now note down loans outstanding, for example, the amount due against a housing loan that you may have taken, and show this on the liabilities' side.

The difference between what you own in the form of assets and what you owe others in the form of liabilities is your capital.

Balance Sheet			
Liabilities		**Assets**	
	Op. bal.		Op. bal.
Capital	72,000	House	1,00,000
		Furniture	8000
		Investments	12,000
Loans:		Jewellery	7000
House Loan	60,000	Bank Balance	5000
	1,32,000		1,32,000

Step 2: List down the receipts

Make a list of all your receipts during the period for which you want to make these statements (let's say for the year). For example:

1. Salary received	29,000
2. Interest earned	7500
3. Dividends received	8500
4. Car loan taken during the year	7500
Total Receipts	**52,500**

Of the total receipts, the first three items should be transferred to the income side of the 'income and expenditure account' (which is similar to a P&L account prepared by business entities).

Income & Expenditure A/C			
Expenses		Income	
		Salary	29,000
		Interest	7500
		Dividends	8500
			45,000

And the fourth item, the car loan, will be shown on the liabilities' side of the balance sheet.

Balance Sheet							
Liabilities				Assets			
	Op. bal.	+/-	Cl. bal.		Op. bal.	+/-	Cl. bal.
Capital	72,000			House	1,00,000		
				Furniture	8000		
Loans:				Investments	12,000		
House Loan	60,000			Jewellery	7000		
Car Loan		7500	7500	Bank Bal	5000		
	1,32,000				1,32,000		

Step 3: List down the expenditures

Now prepare a list of all the expenditures:

1.	School fees paid for the kids	2300
2.	Household expenses	14,000
3.	Money spent on fuel	1500
4.	Income tax paid	3000
5.	Interest paid on the housing loan	6800
6.	Investments made during the year	4000
7.	Television purchased	1200
8.	Housing loan instalment paid	6000
9.	New car purchased	9000
	Total Expenditure	**47,800**

Of the above, the first five items will be shown on the expenses' side of the 'income and expenditure account'.

Income & Expenditure A/C			
Expenses		**Income**	
School fees	2300	Salary	29,000
Household expenses	14,000	Interest	7500
Fuel	1500	Dividend	8500
Income tax	3000		
Interest on loan	6800		
			45,000

And the remaining four, viz.

1.	Investments made during the year	4000
2.	Television purchased	1200
3.	Housing loan instalment paid	6000
4.	New car purchased	9000

. . . will get transferred to the balance sheet.

Balance Sheet

Liabilities	Op. bal.	+/-	Cl. bal.	Assets	Op. bal.	+/-	Cl. bal.
Capital	72,000			House	1,00,000		
				Furniture	8000		
				Investments	12,000	4000	16,000
Loans:				Jewellery	7000		
House Loan	60,000	6000	54,000	Bank Bal	5000		
Car Loan		7500	7500	Television	-	1200	1200
				Car	-	9000	9000
	1,32,000				1,32,000		

Step 4 : Add the difference between receipts and payments to the bank balance

The difference between the total receipts of Rs 52,500 and the total expenditure of Rs 47,800, which works out to Rs 4700, is the net increase to the opening bank balance. This amount will accordingly get added to the bank balance appearing in the opening balance sheet and will now be shown as the closing bank balance.

Balance Sheet

Liabilities	Op. bal.	+/-	Cl. bal.	Assets	Op. bal.	+/-	Cl. bal.
Capital	72,000			House	1,00,000		
				Furniture	8000		
				Investments	12,000	4000	16,000
Loans:				Jewellery	7000		
House Loan	60,000	6000	54,000	Bank Bal	5000	4700	9700
Car Loan		7500	7500	Television	-	1200	1200
				Car	-	9000	9000
	1,32,000				1,32,000		

Step 5: Find out the surplus or deficit

Since the income is in excess of expenses, there is a surplus.

Step 6 : Add the surplus to the opening capital

Balance Sheet							
Liabilities				**Assets**			
	Op. bal.	+/-	Cl. bal.		Op. bal.	+/-	Cl. bal.
Capital	72,000	17,400	89,400	House	1,00,000		
				Furniture	8000		
				Investments	12,000	4000	16,000
Loans:				Jewellery	7000		
House Loan	60,000	6000	54,000	Bank Bal	5000	4700	9700
Car Loan		7500	7500	Television	-	1200	1200
				Car	-	9000	9000
	1,32,000				1,32,000		

This surplus is the accretion to your capital and will accordingly get transferred to the balance sheet and get added to the opening capital.

Now we can show the opening balances of those items which neither had an accretion nor were depleted as the closing balances and complete the balance sheet.

Balance Sheet							
Liabilities				**Assets**			
	Op. bal.	+/-	Cl. bal.		Op. bal.	+/-	Cl. bal.
Capital	72,000	17,400	89,400	House	1,00,000		1,00,000
				Furniture	8000		8000
				Investments	12,000	4000	16,000
Loans:				Jewellery	7000		7000
House Loan	60,000	6000	54,000	Bank Bal	5000	4700	9700
Car Loan		7500	7500	Television	-	1200	1200
				Car	-	9000	9000
	1,32,000		1,50,900		1,32,000		1,50,900

The closing balances in this sheet will be the opening balances for the next period and the process will begin all over again.

‘Money is a guarantee that we may have what we want in the future. Though we need nothing at the moment, it insures the possibility of satisfying a new desire when it arises.’

Aristotle

Chapter 07

Stock Market Investing

Almost inevitably, while addressing a gathering or in conversation at a social event, someone will come up and ask: 'Can you suggest a good investment?' or 'Which scrip would you recommend?' or something to that effect.

Not an easy question to answer at the best of times—not, at least, for somebody with a conscience.

The spectre that haunts the involuntary clairvoyant put in the unenviable position of answering the poser is, what if the advice turns out to be wrong?

In such a scenario it is quite likely that the person you set out in good faith to do a good turn to might catch you by the scruff of your collar in full view of the gathering, similar to the one referred above, and seek an explanation.

I am, of course, only looking at the bleaker side. If the recommendation had turned out to be good and the fellow had made some money, no mention would ever be made of it.

Some of you may recall the days of the past when 'new economy' companies in general, and dotcoms in particular, were a rage not only on NASDAQ, but also on our 'desi' bourses. And all the stock market pundits were predicting continued anti-gravitational movement. Fund managers were also putting their money where their mouths were (therein mingling freely with their feet). The pink and white papers fuelled the bull run by publishing such stories on their front pages. Gullible investors, going by the advice of experts, bet their shirts on such stocks.

Crystal-gazing in the context of stock market investing is indeed a mug's game.

The stock exchange is a market for shares and securities. It is a place where buyers and sellers or their representative brokers meet and enter into deals for purchase and sale of stock and securities.

It is interesting to note that there are two absolutely diverse views about the nature of stock markets. Many people, including some that are well-placed and knowledgeable, think that stock exchanges are gambling dens.

Whereas this may have been partially true about the advent of stock markets, a lot of change has been brought about over the years. Stock exchanges can now be considered to provide reasonably safe avenues of investment, subject of course to the risk an investor is prepared to bear.

A certain amount of speculation still continues with official patronage and is, in a variety of ways, considered good for a stock exchange.

Speculators often lose as they speculate on the day-to-day changes in the prices of more liquid shares.

Unfortunately, the stock exchange is often in the grip of speculators and therefore its behaviour, in the short run, does not always reflect rational decisions.

The temptation to speculate on the stock exchange is very compelling, and this is a pitfall which an average investor must avoid in all circumstances.

A normal investor, however has the full liberty to buy and sell on the stock exchange with no element of speculation therein.

The stock market has been considered by some to be morally depraved, where people presumably participate because, like parlour games and sports, it offers the opportunity to win more dramatically and more concretely than is possible in ordinary work-a-day life.

However, there are others who argue, and quite correctly, that the stock exchange is a vital organ for the economy of the country since it facilitates free movement of capital by providing a market where shares and securities can be bought and sold. Thus, it acts as a channel for employing savings of the people effectively, indirectly helping in rapid industrialization.

It is easier to appreciate the importance of a stock exchange if one visualizes what would happen if there were no such markets. If a person holding shares in a certain company wanted to sell them, he would have to hunt for a buyer informally who would be interested in purchasing this particular stock from out of the millions of investors spread all over the country. In the absence of a market this by itself would be a gigantic task, almost like looking for a needle in a haystack. However, having located a buyer he would have to negotiate, and if necessary bargain, to get a fair price. Similar would be the case if one wanted to buy shares. The stock exchange eliminates all these difficulties by providing a common place and having a mechanism for fixing the prices.

How does one go about investing in shares?

It is a cardinal principle of investment that returns can and should be made only steadily.

There is a direct relationship between return and risk. Anybody who has made quick money on the stock exchange must realize that he has undertaken a great deal of risk unknowingly since a similar practice can result in a disaster in the future.

There is a direct relationship between return and risk. Anybody who has made quick money on the stock exchange must realize that he has undertaken a great deal of risk unknowingly.

However, the long-run price behaviour does reflect the general condition of the economy. It is predictable and reflects inherent economic trends.

Investment decisions basically depend upon the following factors:

1. Objective of investment portfolio

It is important to decide at the very outset what one expects from one's investments. For instance, the manager of a provident fund portfolio has to look for security and would prefer to invest in low-risk securities even though the return may not be high. On the other hand an aggressive investor may be willing to take high risk in order to have high capital appreciation. How the objectives can affect an investment decision can be seen from the fact that most mutual funds have two major schemes. Its capital units are meant for those who wish to have a good capital appreciation and a moderate return. The ordinary units are meant to provide a steady return only. The investment managers under both the schemes will invest the money of the fund in different kinds of shares and securities. Therefore, it is very important that the objectives are clearly defined before an investment decision is taken.

2. Selection of investment

Once the objective of investment is clear, the next step would be to decide upon the kind of investments to be purchased. Selection of investment would involve the following:

(a) Choosing the particular industry which shows a potential for growth.
(b) To select the particular companies in whose shares or securities the investments are to be made.

3. Timing of purchase and sale

The timing of buying and selling of securities is of crucial importance. Even if one can identify correctly the companies in whose shares the investments are to be made, one may lose money if the timing is inappropriate. The price at which the share is acquired for the portfolio depends entirely on the timing decision.

How to identify industries with a high growth potential

First of all, an assessment will have to be made of all the

conditions and factors regarding the demand for the product, cost structure of the industry and other economic and government constraints. An appraisal of the particular industry's prospects is essential since the basic profitability of any company depends upon the prospects of the industry to which it belongs.

The following factors should be taken into consideration while assessing the industry:

a. *Future prospects:* The future prospects of the industry would depend upon the likely demand for products of the industry and the gap between demand and supply. In this regard the investor will have to rely on the various demand forecasts made by agencies like the Planning Commission, chambers of commerce and institutions like the National Council of Applied Economic Research (NCAER). Broadly an industry passes through six identifiable stages during its life time: introduction, development, rapid growth, maturity, saturation and decline. If an industry has already reached the saturation or decline stage, its future demand potential is not likely to be high.

b. *Profitability:* Profitability is a vital factor since it is both a measure of performance as well as a source of earning investors. They may therefore analyse the profitability ratios, especially the return on investment, and the gross profit ratio of the existing companies in the industry. This would give them an idea about the profitability of the industry as a whole. All this information, and much more, can easily be obtained from financial and business publications, as well as through a basic search using the Internet.

c. *Particular characteristics of the industry:* Each industry has its own characteristics which must be studied in depth, in order to understand their impact on the working of the industry. For example, certain industries have a fast-changing technology. In such industries technological obsolescence will take place at a fast rate. Similarly, many other industries are characterized by cyclical fluctuation in profits and losses which must be carefully studied.

d. ***Labour management relations in the industry:*** The state of relations between the labour and management in the industry also has a great deal of the influence on its future profitability. Investors should check to see whether or not cordial relations have been maintained.
Once the industries with growth potential have been identified, the next step would be to analyse the companies within the industry and choose those which are desirable from investment point of view.

Company analysis

A company's growth potential can be roughly judged by studying its past performance. However, one should keep in mind that past performance and information is relevant only to the extent that it extends to the future trends. An illustrative list of factors that an analyst should take into consideration are as follows:

1. Size and ranking: A rough idea of the size and ranking of the company within the economy in general, and the industry in particular, would help the investor in assessing the risk associated with the company. In this regard, the net capital employed, the net profits, the return on investment and the sales figures of the company under consideration may be compared with the similar data of the companies in the same industry group. It may also be useful to assess the position of the company in terms of technical know-how and research and development.

2. Growth record: The growth in sales, net income, net capital employed and earnings per share of the company in the past few years should be examined. The following three growth indicators may be particularly looked into:

a) Price to earnings ratio,
b) Percentage growth rate of earnings per annum and
c) Percentage growth rate of net block.

3. Financial analysis: An analysis of its financial statements for the past few years, with the help of certain fundamental ratios, would help the investor in understanding the financial solvency and liquidity, the efficiency with which the funds are used, the profitability and the operating efficiency.

4. Quality of management: This is an intangible factor with a very important bearing on the value of the shares. Every investor knows that shares of certain business houses command a higher premium than those of similar companies managed by other business houses. This is because of the quality of management, the confidence that the investors have in a particular business house, its policy vis-à-vis relationship with the investors, dividend and financial performance record of other companies in the same group, etc. The quality of management has to be seen with reference to the experience, skills and integrity of the persons at the helm of affairs of the company. The policy of the management regarding the relationship with shareholders is an important factor since certain business houses believe in very generous dividends and bonus distributions while others are rather conservative.

Other factors to be kept in mind are the location of the company's manufacturing facilities, the labour-management relations, the pattern of existing stock holdings and the marketability of the shares, the speculative interest in the particular scrip, the particular stock exchange where it is traded and the volume of trading.

Timing your entry and exit

The decision regarding timing of purchases is particularly difficult because of certain psychological factors.

It is quite obvious that if one wishes to make any gains, one should 'buy cheap and sell dear', that is, buy when the shares are selling at a low price and sell when they are at a high price.

Although this sounds easy, in practice it is very difficult. An ordinary investor, on the contrary, normally buys when the prices have risen and sells when they have fallen. When the prices are rising in the share market, everybody joins in the buying spree since the general environment is one of confidence.

Those who delay buying regret it, as everyday prices touch a new high. The ordinary investor joins the buying rush when it is in full steam and therefore usually buys the shares at a high price.

When the downturn begins, an atmosphere of despondency pervades.

The ordinary investor gets panicky and as every day the prices fall and reach a new low, he regrets why he did not sell his shares the previous day. Ultimately, he sells the shares at a substantial loss, thanking his stars that he has gone out of the market.

This kind of an investment decision is essentially devoid of a sense of timing.

The reason why timing is important is because the most likely prospect is that the existing trend will continue. But the greatest profits come when trends change.

If a share is going up, it is most likely to continue going up. Yet it is the investor, who judges when it has reached the top and then sells, who will get the best price.

An investor has to view the problem of investment as one of buying and selling over a period during which sometimes the markets are in bull phases, i.e. the prices are rising, and sometimes the markets are in bear phases, i.e. the prices are falling, and at other times the markets are stagnant, i.e. there is no significant trend of rise or fall in prices.

Investments are to be purchased when prices are low and sold when prices are high. This requires swimming against the general current in the market. Hence, there must be an in-built system of timing the purchases or sale of investments so that the psychological factors are

ignored and purchases are made when the prices are entering the bull phase and sold when they are entering the bear phase.

Investments are to be purchased when prices are low and sold when prices are high. This requires swimming against the general current in the market.

If a graph is prepared of the share market prices and fluctuations therein, one would notice that the prices rise for a certain time, say for a year or two, and then fall and remain low for a year or two.

The best way to study the share market prices is to watch the share price index. The BSE Sensex (The S&P Bombay Stock Exchange Sensitive Index) and NSE NIFTY 50 (Standard And Poor's CNX Nifty) are two important indices that investors regularly use in India.

Dow Jones Theory

The Dow Jones Theory is probably the most popular theory regarding the behaviour of stock market prices, deriving its name from Charles H. Dow who established Dow Jones & Company and was the first editor of the Wall Street Journal, a leading publication on financial and economic matters in the USA.

This theory classifies the movements of prices on the share market into three broad categories: the primary movements, the secondary movements and the daily fluctuations.

The primary movements reflect the trend of the stock market and last from one to three or more years. If one observes the long-range behaviour of the stock market prices, it will be observed that the share markets go into definite phases where the prices consistently rise or fall, that is, the bull or the bear phase.

Graph 1

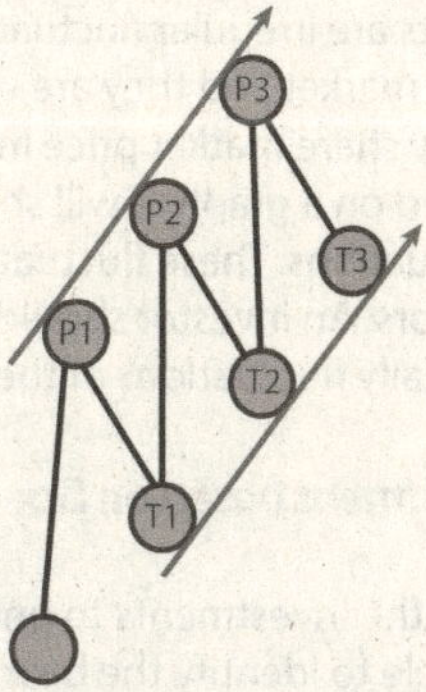

Graph 1 depicts a bull phase where the basic trend is that of a rise in prices. That is each trough and peak that the prices reach is at a higher level than the earlier one. Thus, P2 is higher than P1 and T2 is higher than T1. Similarly, **graph 2** shows a bear phase where the trend is of a fall in prices.

Graph 2

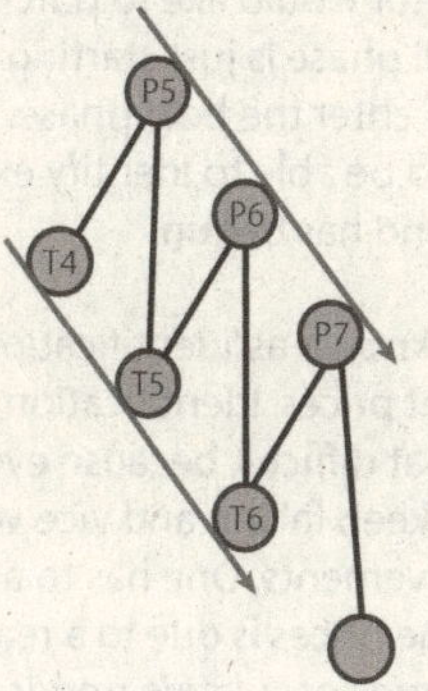

One can observe that even when the market is in a bull phase, after each rise in the prices, there is a fall. Similarly in a bear phase, one can notice a rise in prices after each fall. Therefore even though the primary trend is that of a consistent rise and fall in the former and latter cases respectively, there are small movements in the opposite direction also. These movements are known as secondary movements and are shorter in duration. These movements last anywhere between three weeks to three months and retrace one-third to two-thirds of the previous advance in the bull market or previous fall in the bear market.

Daily movements are irregular fluctuations which occur every day in the market and they are without any definite trend. If the daily share market price index for a few months is plotted on a graph, it will show both upward and downward fluctuations. These fluctuations are the result of speculative factors. An investor should scrupulously keep away from the daily fluctuations of the market.

Timing of investment based on Dow Jones Theory

In order to time the investments to one's best advantage, one has to be able to identify the bear and bull phases. As indicated above, the primary movements indicate the basic phase trend in the market. If the cyclical swings of the stock market price indications are successfully higher, the market trend is up and there is a bull market trend. On the other hand, if the 'highs' and 'lows' are successfully lower, there is a downward trend and we are in a bear market. Ideally speaking, an investor would like to purchase the shares at a time when the bull phase is just starting and sell when the market is about to enter the bear phase. This means that the investor should be able to identify exactly when the falling or rising trend has begun.

This is technically known as 'identification of the turn' in the share market prices. Identification of these turns becomes somewhat difficult because even in a rising market the prices keep falling and vice versa, as a result of the secondary movements. One has to ascertain whether the rise or fall in the prices is due to a real turn in prices or only due to short run speculative trends.

The Dow Jones Theory identifies the turn in the market prices by seeing whether the successive rises and falls are higher or lower than earlier.

Consider **graph 3**. According to the theory, the investor should purchase the investments when the prices are at T2. At this point, he can know that one bull trend has started since T2 is higher than T1 and P2 is higher than P1. Similarly, when the prices reach P6, he should sell. At this point he can know that the bearish trend has started, since P6 is lower than P5 and T5 is lower than T4.

Graph 3

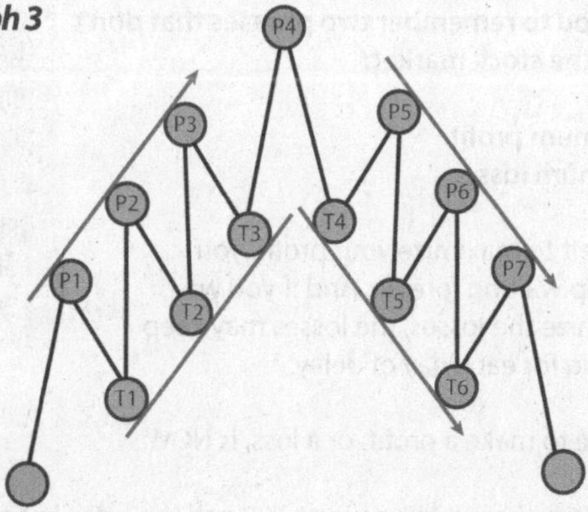

Stock market investment strategy

There are many investment strategies to choose from.

Let me share with you one of many.

Let's imagine, after doing the industry research and the company analysis, you purchased 1000 shares of a particular company at the rate of Rs 100 each making a total investment of Rs 1,00,000.

Before you even think of the profit that you can make, you must decide the loss you are willing to suffer and put a stop-loss limit.

You may decide that you do not want to lose more than Rs 10 per share. That is, in case the price of this share falls to Rs 90, you will sell and get out. And you will not regret it if the price bounces back up.

But since you have done your study and timed your entry as discussed above, there is a greater chance that the price will move upward. Let's say a little later the price increases to Rs 120.

What should you do now?

I want you to remember two phrases that don't exist in the stock market:

1. Maximum profit
2. Minimum loss.

I want you to remember two phrases that don't exist in the stock market:
1. Maximum profit
2. Minimum loss.

If you wait to maximize your profit, you may keep waiting forever. And if you wait to minimize the losses, the losses may keep mounting for each day of delay.

The time to make a profit, or a loss, is NOW.

You had purchased this scrip at 100 and the price has now moved up to Rs 120. What should you do?

Sell a hundred shares at Rs 120.

Why only 100 and not the entire lot?

That is because if the price moves up further, you have more shares to sell. And in case it drops to below Rs 100, you will lose less since the average cost of the remaining 900 shares is now lower than Rs 100. (Remember this is merely one of many strategies).

A little later, the price increases to Rs 140.

Sell another 100.

The price goes up to Rs 160.
Sell another 100.
The price now falls to Rs 150.

What should you do?

Buy back what you sold at 160 (provided the original logic applied at the time of buying the initial lot still holds).
Why should you buy it back?

You have sold the stock at Rs 160 and purchased it back at Rs 150. The shares are back with you and you have pocketed a profit of Rs 1000. What more can you ask for?

At every rise you must sell, at every fall buy back. Unless the price falls to Rs 90, at which point you must sell the entire lot and get out; remember?

In fact, the stop-loss must also be revised once you see the price has gone up first to Rs 120 and then to Rs 140. Why should you now be willing to lose anything at all? Maybe you should decide that you will sell the entire lot and exit if the price falls to Rs 110. Above Rs 110, at every rise you must sell and at every fall buy back.

Keep profits open-ended and put a stop-loss.

People often tend to do the reverse. They put a limit on the profit and keep their losses open-ended.

If the scrip that they have invested in appreciates a certain percentage points, they sell the entire lot, satisfied with the profit made. And if the price continues rising thereafter, they have no shares left to sell. However, if the price falls below what they have paid for it, they keep hoping and praying that it will bounce back.

Keep profits open-ended and put a stop-loss.

People often tend to do the reverse. They put a limit on the profit and keep their losses open-ended.

If you follow this as a rule, it will serve you well.

Word of caution: Don't let your portfolio become too unwieldy. There are some who don't invest in stocks at all. Others go overboard, having 100 to 150 scrips in the portfolio. Nobody can be right every time.

If you have such a large portfolio, at the best of times, half the scrips that you hold may be looking up and the other half down.

In my opinion, the number of scrips in the portfolio should be in single digits. This way relatively large sums of money can be invested in each and the amount of investment will Justify spending more time on researching the stock well and also monitoring its price movements.

'Too many people spend money they haven't earned, to buy things they don't want, to impress people that they don't like.'

Will Rogers

Chapter 08

Investing Through Mutual Funds

What are mutual funds?

Many people shy away from investing in stocks and bonds despite wanting to because they don't understand how to go about it. They may not have the time to study the market and the fundamentals of the companies or may have some other reasons.

For such people an ideal way would be to invest through mutual funds.

If a large number of individuals, who do not possess the expertise or are too busy to invest individually, pool in their money into a fund and the fund invests in stocks, bonds, money market instruments and other assets on their behalf, it becomes a mutually beneficial exercise. Since the amount becomes reasonably large, the fund can afford to hire professional money managers on a full-time basis, who take investment decisions for the fund and allocate its investments with a view to earn capital gains and/or regular income for the investors.

The fund charges the investors a small fee for managing the money.

The expenses incurred by the mutual fund are collectively called expense ratio which generally vary between 1.5–2.5 per cent of the average weekly net assets of the schemes.

Just as there are shares in companies, in a mutual fund one purchases units.

If you take the market value of the portfolio of assets that the fund has invested in less its liabilities and divide it by the number of units, you arrive at the per unit **NAV** or the **Net Asset Value.**

NAV is calculated at the end of every market day, after taking into account the closing market prices of the portfolio's securities. For example, if a fund has assets of Rs 60 million and liabilities of Rs 10 million, it would have a net asset value of Rs 50 million. If you divide the NAV of a fund by the number of outstanding units, you get the price per unit. In our example, if the fund had 5 million shares outstanding, the price-per-unit value would be 10 (that is 50 million divided by 5 million).

This is the price at which investors buy units from a fund company or sell it back to the fund house. The NAV of a fund is calculated by the mutual fund house itself or by an accounting firm hired by the mutual fund.

Different schemes having higher or lower NAVs. Neither reflect on the fund's current performance in any way, nor the profit that can be made by investing in them. So a unit of a certain scheme available at an NAV of Rs 10 may not be less profitable than another one being sold at Rs 100. It would simply indicate that for a certain amount of investment to be made you would be able to acquire a larger number of units of the former as compared to the latter. If the NAV of the units purchased at Rs 10 increases to Rs 12 and of the other one to Rs 110, the value of the investment has appreciated by 20 per cent in the first case and by 10 per cent in the second case.

Daily changes in the NAV of mutual fund schemes do not matter. It would be better to look at the annualized return of a fund over different time frames to judge its performance.

Types of mutual funds

In India, the Securities and Exchange Board of India (SEBI) has categorized mutual funds broadly into four categories:

1. Equity mutual funds:
These funds invest directly in stocks. Since equity markets are prone to fluctuations, these are high-risk, high-return schemes. These are useful for investors having a longer-term investment horizon of over five years.

2. Debt mutual funds:
These schemes invest in debt securities. Since debt is

not subject to the vagaries of market fluctuations, these schemes are stable and substantially safe, but also provide mediocre returns. These funds would appeal to those looking to invest for short periods of less than five years.

3. Hybrid mutual funds:
These funds invest their money in a combination of equity and debt. The schemes of such funds provide returns which are higher than pure debt funds.

4. Solution-oriented mutual funds:
These mutual funds offer schemes for specific needs or purposes like children's education or for post-retirement. These schemes usually have a lock-in period of five years.

What is a systematic investment plan?

A smart way of investing in mutual funds is through a systematic investment plan or SIP.

SIPs allow you to invest a certain fixed amount at regular intervals of your choice—weekly, monthly, quarterly, etc.

It helps investors inculcate the habit of saving in a planned manner.

In case of an SIP, the money gets debited from your bank account on a standing instruction and gets invested into mutual fund schemes. The number of units that get allocated depends on the NAV on that day.

For each instalment of investment, additional units of the scheme are purchased at the market rate and added to your account. Over a period of time, since units are purchased at different rates, the investors get the benefit of rupee-cost averaging and also the power of compounding works to their advantage.

Cost averaging

Most people understand that one should buy a commodity when the price comes down and sell when the price goes up. But they end up doing the opposite when it comes to investing in equity.

In the absence of a SIP, one would have to apply one's mind to time one's entry and exit from the market. In volatile markets this becomes difficult. Cost averaging allows you to eliminate this uncertainty. An SIP investor, while investing every month, would end up buying more units when markets go down and buying less units when the market goes up. It would help in achieving a lower average cost per unit.

Power of compounding

The power of compound interest has been called the most powerful force in the universe.

You can make compounding work for you by:

1. Beginning the saving habit as early as possible and
2. Saving regularly.

SIPs help you develop the habit of regular saving.

> 'Buy at the point of maximum pessimism; sell at the point of maximum optimism.'
>
> Sir John Templeton

Chapter 09

Taxprudence

What is income tax?
Why do we pay taxes?
Should we pay income tax?

Let me try and answer some such questions.

What is income tax?

A straightforward interpretation would be that it is a tax on income. So to understand income tax, we need to understand these two words—tax and income.

What is tax and what is income?

What is a tax? Any tax?

A tax is a levy, it is a statutory, mandatory payment made to the government. And therefore, what is income tax? When the amount to be paid is a percentage of the income, it is called income tax.

When we pay to the government a percentage of the value of goods manufactured, it is called excise duty. When it is a percentage of goods entering into the country, it is called customs duty. When it is a percentage of the value of goods entering a city—octroi. When it is a percentage of the value of goods sold—VAT. Percentage of the value of services rendered—service tax. (Most of these have now been replaced by the GST—the Goods and Service Tax—in India)

We keep paying the government in a variety of ways. Yet another way in which we pay is when it is a percentage of our income. Then the tax is called income tax. The critical word to be understood is 'income'. Unless you know what is 'income' you will not be able to work out the income tax payable.

So, what is 'income' from the point of view of income tax?

People have a number of misconceptions when it comes to defining income.

'Income' is something broader than mere earnings and not as broad as to cover all receipts.

One response is that 'income' is everything that comes in—all the receipts of money. But this is too broad a definition. Many receipts do not constitute income. For example, a loan taken from a bank brings money in but is obviously not 'income'. Also inheritances are not considered 'income'. Nor are gifts, under certain circumstances.

Another reaction is that 'income' refers to earnings. But unearned receipts, such as winnings from lottery or lucky draws, are also 'income' subject to income tax.

So 'income' is something broader than mere earnings and not as broad as to cover all receipts.

Yet another misconception is that legal earnings are 'income' and illegally obtained money is not.

The truth is that 'income' for the purposes of income tax covers almost all the money coming in, barring a few specific exceptions like loans, and gifts (in some cases) and inheritances. It does not matter whether it is earned or unearned, legal or illegal, received or accrued.

Should we pay income tax?

It doesn't matter how much it may hurt people to pay taxes, whenever I ask this question, invariably the answer is 'Of course, we should pay.'

What really hurts people is not so much the paying as the misuse of the money paid. If people were sure that the taxes paid will actually be used for the purpose for which they were collected, more people would pay happily.

Why do we pay taxes?

Taxes are obviously paid so that governments can raise the resources to pay for the various facilities provided for us but which none of us can provide for ourselves individually.

Even if I don't go into complicated theories of taxation and take some blatant examples of services and amenities that the government provides—roads, street lighting, police, the army—all of which are of a nature that it is neither possible nor affordable for citizens of a country to obtain on their own. I mean, if the government asks all of us to build a road for, say, a 100 metres outside our respective houses, a majority of us will not be able to afford it. But how many miles and miles of roads do we use? We use postal services. We use the railways (which so far in India is in government hands). The police is there to protect us. Without the army guarding our borders we probably would be slaves to some marauding and ambitious rogue nation.

So, the logic of income tax (as other taxes) is that, all of us use the facilities and hence all of us must pay.

The problem of income tax is—all of us use the facilities, but all of us don't pay. Not only that all of us don't pay, but all of us can't pay.

And why can't all of us pay?

This is because a large percentage of our population lives below what is known as the poverty line.

What does it mean when we say that someone is living BPL (below the poverty line)?

I often ask this question in my talks. How much does a BPL person earn?

And the answer very often is that a person living below the poverty line does not earn enough to be able to provide the basic needs of life.

And what are the basic needs? The answer to this question many times is food, clothing and shelter.

The truth is that a person living below the poverty line does not earn enough to have three meals a day. Some estimate is made by someone sitting in the Planning Commission or some such government department, that what should be the calorie intake per day of a normally healthy individual in order to continue to remain healthy. This figure differs based on whether one is living in urban or rural areas; some say 2100 and 2400 calories per day respectively, the latter having to do more physical work.

The next calculation is to work out what it costs to acquire enough food to get that many calories. This number was a ridiculous Rs 10 for rural and Rs 15 per day for urban areas (Rs 328 and Rs 454 per month, that is about $5 and $7 per month) in the year 2000. The Tendulkar Committee revised this number to Rs 27 and Rs 33 (in 2009) and the C. Ranjan Committee raised it to Rs 32 and Rs 47 respectively in 2014.

Any person earning less than this is considered to be living below the poverty line. And if there is a family of four, then multiply this figure by 4, and if the family income is below that number, it is said to be a BPL family.

Even conservative government estimates put the percentage of our population that lives below the poverty line at around 30. Privately one even hears of a percentage as high as 50.

I said earlier that the logic of collecting tax is that all of us enjoy the facilities, therefore all of us must pay. Can this 50 per cent afford to pay? Are they even bothered whether the roads have potholes and whether the street lights are functioning effectively or not. They are struggling merely to survive.

(Often, some people move above the line not because they start earning more but because the line moves lower, after being redefined. Or it also happens that incomes increase marginally, but due to inflation prices move up by a bigger percentage. Even though, effectively speaking, one may be poorer than before, but a look at the income figures in isolation may make it appear that one is better off than earlier).

That leaves us with the remaining 50 per cent, the ones that are above the line.

Now, so far as income tax is concerned, the government's stand is that it doesn't want you to pay income tax unless you lead a relatively decent life. The figure that will enable you to lead a fairly comfortable life in India is at present pegged by the government at Rs 250,000 per annum. That is, Rs 2,50,000 per annum per earning member of a family.

So, if a family has ten members, each earning Rs 2,50,000 annually, the family income would be Rs 2.5 million and the income tax collected by the government would be ZERO.

Out of the 50 per cent that are APL (above the poverty line), perhaps 40 per cent earn less than the minimum required to pay income tax.

Now we are left with some 10 per cent of the population that is not only APL but has a surplus above Rs 2,50,000 out of which they can pay income tax.

And of this 10 per cent, about 70 per cent are tax evaders.

(These percentages are not exact but approximations and are merely intended to be illustrative).

Do you see how grave the situation is?

A while ago I had posed a question: 'Should we pay taxes?'

In my opinion, any attempt at evading, or even saving, taxes is probably more expensive than the payment of tax itself.

My answer is, of course, we should. If for no other reason than as a token of thanksgiving that we happen to occupy the top 2–3 per cent slot of this nation's population, the least we can do is pay our taxes honestly.

And I'm not sermonizing. I think it is the most practical thing to do. In my opinion, any attempt at evading, or even saving, taxes is probably more expensive than the payment of tax itself.

Why it makes sense to pay taxes

To understand why it makes sense for all of us to pay taxes, we must first understand from where and how the government gets its money and how it is spent.

Each year the government presents a budget, which lists out the expected receipts and expenditure for the coming fiscal year.

A country's receipts are chiefly comprised of two components: earnings and borrowings (or revenue receipts and capital receipts).

Governments earn money from taxes (both direct and indirect).

A nation's borrowings can be further categorized as internal and external.

When you and I deposit money in a PPF account or invest in National Savings Certificates or even buy an insurance policy from the Life Insurance Corporation of India, we have lent money to the government (internal borrowings).

Loans taken from the International Monetary Fund (IMF), the World Bank and others similar institutions constitute external borrowings.

The government's spending appears to be independent of its income.

Similarly, expenditures are classified as revenue and capital expenditures. The former comprises expenses of running the government, payment of salaries, maintaining the police force and the army, and, of course, interest on loans taken. The latter includes developmental expenditure, that on construction of roads, bridges, and airports and so on.

The government's spending appears to be independent of its income.

I often get the feeling that the persons in charge of spending and those responsible for generating receipts are separate groups, perhaps not on talking terms with each other. Consequently, the balance between receipts and expenditures is rarely achieved.

If the planned receipts and the planned expenditures match, the budget is called a 'balanced' budget; if the receipts exceed the expenditures, it would be a 'surplus' budget; and if the budgeted expenditures are greater than the budgeted receipts, it would be called a 'deficit' budget.

I don't think any of us will recall seeing the first two types of budgets—the balanced and the surplus types. What we get to see year after year after year are 'deficit' budgets.

What is the fundamental difference between budgets made by you and I and the ones made by the government?

You and I cannot have deficits, but governments can.

What do I mean by that?

Why can't we have deficit budgets?

Can't we earn Rs 100 and spend Rs 120?

Yes, we can; we can borrow Rs 20.

But what we cannot do is spend more than what we earn AND what we borrow.

A government's deficit budget means its spending exceeds both earnings AND borrowings.

How can it do that?

It can do that because the government also happens to own the country's printing presses.

So, when it finds that it needs to spend, and doesn't have the money to do so, orders go out to the printing press to print more currency notes.

When governments create money to meet expenditure, that phenomenon is called 'deficit financing.'

For price to go up or down there has to be a unilateral increase in either demand or supply.

Do you and I pay a price for this tendency of the government to print money to spend?

Yes, we do. **The fallout of deficit financing is inflation.**

Why is deficit financing inflationary?

Just because the government needed to spend and it created money to do so, why does it lead to an increase in the price of the bread at the bakery?

This is because price is a function of demand and supply. If the demand for a commodity goes up, the price goes up, unless it is accompanied by an equivalent increase in the supply of that commodity too. And vice versa. If the supply of something increases, the price falls, unless there is a corresponding increase in the buying power.

For price to go up or down there has to be a unilateral increase in either demand or supply.

When the buying power of a people goes up because they have worked harder and therefore earned more, it is non-inflationary. This is because their buying power has increased by producing more goods and services. So, if on the one hand there is more money to spend, on the other there are also more goods and services to buy.

However, when the government prints money and spends, there is merely an increase in the supply of money, without an increase in the supply of goods. More money is now chasing the same quantity of goods and is therefore inflationary.

Why should we pay taxes?

I had mentioned earlier that a government's spending is independent of its receipts.

It makes a certain estimate of where the money will come from and where it will be spent.

Let's say, the government expected to collect 'x' amount from income tax. And, due to tax evasion on the part of some people, the government actually collects less than 'x'. Do you think it will not spend?

If income tax collection falls short, it will introduce another tax. If direct tax collection is insufficient, it will increase the rate of some indirect tax.

What is the difference between a direct and an indirect tax?

Direct taxes are those which, if you have to pay, are collected by the government from you. e.g. income tax. Indirect taxes are those which you pay to someone else and that person pays it to the government (e.g. goods and services tax).

I would any day prefer to pay direct over indirect taxes. This is because direct taxes can be collected according to the ability to pay. For instance, take income tax. The government can tell one person, your income is too low and there is no need to pay anything and tell another person, since you are relatively richer, you must pay at a higher rate to make up for those who can't.

However, indirect taxes hit everyone uniformly. If you buy something from a grocery shop and pay Rs 10 as GST, a beggar wishing to buy the same item will also have to pay Rs 10.

And if the government still cannot manage to collect the required amount, it will resort to printing of notes which will result in inflation and reduction in the value of our money.

What I'm trying to say is that eventually it is you and I that have to pay. And if we have to pay anyway, then the cheapest and the best way of paying was the original way in which we were supposed to pay.

So, attempting to save, and definitely evade, taxes is

actually a mug's game. One has spent all that time and energy (and most likely lost one's peace of mind in the process too) and in the end gained nothing.

There is an even more sinister dimension to tax evasion, which I will dwell upon a little later.

The brighter side of taxation

Up till now I have painted a very bleak picture of the tax situation illustrating how just a minuscule percentage of the population pays taxes.

Let me now show you the brighter side of the picture.

Let's take the case of income tax alone. I receive income and I pay tax on it. What do I do with this money? I have needs. Let's say I am a salaried person and I have been waiting to receive my salary so that I can purchase a shirt for myself. I receive my salary, pay income tax, and then go and spend this money on a shirt. This money goes from my pocket to the pocket of the shirt seller. It becomes the shirt seller's income. She pays tax on it. Maybe, she has been wanting to buy a pair of shoes. When she spends this money, it becomes the shoe seller's income. The shoe seller pays tax on it. Do you realize each time a rupee merely changes hands it becomes somebody's income and the government gets a share of it?

It has been estimated that out of every rupee that is made, more than 97 paise goes back to the government by way of income tax alone. (Once I was thinking aloud, why only 97 paise? Why not Rs 5? And someone pointed out, that is probably because by the time 97 paise get collected, the rupee must be getting worn out and discarded).

And this is income tax alone. I earn a rupee, I pay income tax. If I use that money to purchase an asset, and if I still own that asset on March 31, it becomes part of my wealth on which I must pay wealth tax. And having paid income tax and wealth tax, a little later, in one of my generous moods, if I gift the item to somebody, I would have had to pay gift tax. And a little later, if I happen to die, somebody on my behalf would have needed to pay estate duty on the wealth left behind by me.

Mercifully in India, many years ago, estate duty was abolished. Subsequently, donor-based gift tax also got abolished (and a milder version in the form of donee-based income tax on gifts received in certain circumstances was later introduced). Wealth tax provisions were diluted to such an extent that a far smaller percentage than before are now liable to pay it. The formula to calculate long-term capital gains was tweaked to introduce the concept of cost inflation index that substantially reduced the tax on capital gains. The tax rates on long-term capital gains were also reduced. The highest marginal tax rate, which in the 1960s was a ridiculous 98 per cent, and even at the start of the liberalization process in 1991 was 60 and 55 per cent respectively for corporate and personal taxpayers, was reduced to 30 per cent. Today, taxpayers in India really do not have any reason to complain.

Tax planner vs tax evader

Taxpayers can broadly be classified into two types: tax planners and tax evaders.

Who is a tax planner? What is a tax planner trying to achieve? A tax planner is a person who is trying to arrange the affairs in such a way that the tax liability gets minimized or eliminated.

What is a tax evader attempting to do? Also trying to minimize or eliminate the tax liability.

The end result of the actions of both is that the government loses tax revenue. But the former is considered to be a respectable citizen and the latter a crook.

Why is that so?

The difference obviously lies in the method adopted by them.

How does a tax planner save taxes?

The Income Tax Act provides several avenues of saving money which give tax relief. For instance, Section 80-C of the Income Tax Act provides that if a taxpayer invests in certain specified avenues, for instance, pays life insurance premium or invests in certain mutual fund schemes, the tax liability can go down, subject to certain limits.
How did the tax planner save tax? By saving and investing money, by taking a life insurance policy, etc.
But shouldn't any rational person be doing this anyhow? Shouldn't people be saving for a rainy day and protecting their loved ones by insuring themselves irrespective of whether the government gives them tax deduction or not?

Is the government a net loser in this bargain?

Why does the government say that if you do something that you should be doing anyhow, we will sacrifice a certain amount of income tax?

Is the government a net loser or must it also be gaining?

Obviously, it must be gaining too.

The government not only wants you to save, but also wants to channelize your savings into certain specific areas.

If you purchase a National Saving Certificate, the money comes to the government for five years; for fifteen years or more if you invest in a PPF account; perhaps for twenty years if you take an insurance policy from the Life Insurance Corporation of India, and so on.

What can the government do with this money?

They can further lend it through public financial institutions to industry, which in turn would lead to more employment, more production, more development, more growth in the GDP.

Some calculation must be made by the government as to what it will cost the exchequer to induce taxpayers to save in these areas (loss of tax revenue of up to 30 per cent of the amount invested), and what the gain to the nation will be.

The deduction would be provided only if this cost-benefit analysis revealed a net gain to the government.

What I'm trying to say is that when a tax planner saves tax, both the tax planner and the nation are gainers.

It would be misplaced patriotism for a person to say, 'I am a patriot, I don't want my country to lose any taxes, therefore I am not going to save a single rupee and pay full taxes.' It is a moot point whether this person has done a service or a disservice to the nation.

How does a tax evader save taxes?

The modus operandi adopted by a tax evader not to pay taxes is merely to stay quiet and not reveal the income earned.

In my opinion the very fact that a tax evader does not pay taxes is a minor crime (even the tax planner did not pay taxes). But this minor crime necessarily leads to a major crime.

The cancerous tendencies of black money

The tax evader has to essentially be a very intelligent person otherwise he will soon get caught.

And how will he get caught?

Because if this money is used to acquire an expensive property, a luxury car, membership to an exclusive club or other such items, sooner or later he is likely to receive an income tax notice asking to explain the source from where these were purchased.

Therefore, the avenues of spending for a tax evader get substantially reduced.

When the tax evader realizes that he has the money and is scared to spend it for fear of being detected, this money then finds its way under the tile in his bathroom.

And here is where the bigger crime begins.

What is the bigger crime?

Both the tax planner and evader have not paid taxes.

But the tax planner is not scared to spend.

The fact that the tax evader did not pay taxes is, as said earlier, a minor crime.

But the tax evader does not spend to avoid detection. He starts hoarding the money.

By not spending, the tax evader has not only deprived the nation of the tax that he should have paid, but also of the tax that countless people after him would have paid.

And this is where the bigger crime starts. He breaks the chain.

Remember, one person earns money and pays income tax. When this money is spent, it becomes the recipient's income, who again pays tax. When this person spends, it becomes the next person's income. If that person does not pay tax, I say it is a minor crime. But when that person does not spend (for fear of being caught) it leads to the bigger crime.

By not spending, the tax evader has not only deprived the nation of the tax that he should have paid, but also of the tax that countless people after him would have paid.

And it spreads like cancer.

It's not that the tax evader does not spend. From his bathroom it goes to somebody else's bathroom.
Hoarding money at home is not without its fair share of

risk. What if an income tax raid takes place? How will this money be explained? So, the taxpayer perhaps approaches a builder to purchase some property, but offers to pay a large portion in cash. The builder then uses that money to purchase land and makes a similar offer to the land seller.

So, the money moves, but it moves in parallel circles. And therefore, the black economy is also called the parallel economy. However the nation, and by extension you and I, get no benefit out of it.

Voluntary disclosure schemes

Which is why periodically governments come out with amnesty and voluntary disclosure schemes.

I have always felt that all such schemes are poignant statements coming from the government. It is as if the government is telling the tax evaders: 'You and we have been playing a game of cops and robbers. Your job was to evade taxes and ours to try and catch you. We admit defeat. You win and we lose. If you don't want to pay taxes, don't. But please start spending this money and allow others to pay. And if you are scared to do so, we assure you that we will do nothing to you for these misdemeanours of yours.'

How to calculate taxable income

The Income Tax Act imposes two obligations on the citizens:

1. Pay your taxes
2. Tell us how you arrived at the amount paid (called the filing of returns).

Income tax returns are filed at the income tax office.

Three ways to pay income tax

Income tax is paid in three ways:

1. Tax Deduction at Source (TDS): Even though it is the primary responsibility of the person earning the income to pay tax, the law, in certain cases, imposes an additional responsibility on the payer of the income to deduct tax at the source itself and pay the balance to the recipient. The logic being that the probability of compliance is far greater since it does not pinch the payer to deduct the tax and pay it to the government.

2. Advance Tax: The Income Tax Act expects taxpayers to be clairvoyants to a certain extent, and to be able to anticipate the income to be earned up to the end of the year and pay the tax due on that income by way of advance tax. For any year ending on March 31, advance tax is to be paid in three instalments on or before September 15, December 15 and March 15. (Corporate assessees have to pay in four instalments).

3. Self-Assessment Tax: Once the accounting year has come to an end, one is now in a position to know the correct tax liability since there is clarity about the income earned over the previous twelve months. In case the eventual tax liability is greater than the tax already paid to the government by way of TDS as well as advance tax, the difference has to be paid by way of self-assessment tax along with interest, which is kind of a penalty for inadequate clairvoyance abilities.

How to Compute Taxable Income (called Total Income)

Five heads of income

For calculation of the taxable income, all income earned, no matter from how many different sources, must get classified into a maximum of five different heads.

1. **Income from salaries**
2. **Income from house property**
3. **Profits and gains of business or profession**

4. Capital gains and
5. Income from other sources

Let me give you a few steps to arrive at the total income

Step I: Compute the NET INCOME from the various heads

Step II: Add the NET INCOMES to arrive at the GROSS TOTAL INCOME

Step III: Claim deductions available under Chapter VIA or Section 80 of the Income Tax Act and arrive at the TOTAL INCOME

Step IV: Arrive at the tax liability by applying the slab rates of income tax

Step V: Compare the tax liability so arrived at with the pre-assessment taxes paid (by way of TDS and advance tax). If exuces has been paid, claim a refund, and if there is a shortfall it should be paid by way self-assessment tax before filing the return of income.

Let us now discuss each of these steps

STEP I: Compute the NET INCOME from the various heads

1. Income from salaries

In normal connotation, salary is interpreted as the amount received by an employee from an employer for services rendered. However, for the purpose of calculating income tax, salary includes basic salary, DA, bonus, pension, gratuity, commission, any advance salary, taxable portion of allowances and the value of perquisites received by the employee, if any.

From the gross salary so computed, employees are permitted two deductions:

i) A standard deduction of Rs 40,000 or the amount of salary received, whichever is less and

ii) The tax on employment paid by the employee.

The balance amount is the **NET INCOME FROM SALARIES.**

2. Income from house property

Owners of house properties are expected to compute income from such properties and the amount so arrived at is to be added to their other incomes.

A layman's understanding of income from house property would be that unless a person owns a house property and lets it out, there would be no question of any income there from. But here lies the difference between the layman and the taxman. A taxman would point out to you that such minor issues as not having any actual income have never come in the way of collecting taxes, and the Income Tax Act provides that income from house property would have to be calculated irrespective of whether the property has been let out (in which case there would be genuine income) or is self-occupied (where income would be calculated on a notional basis).

However, with respect to one self-occupied house property, the income will be deemed to be nil. If an assessee owns more than one self-occupied property, such properties are treated as **deemed to be let-out properties** and income is to be calculated on a notional basis.

Thus house properties get classified into three categories:

a. Let out properties
b. Self-occupied property (i.e. one property at the choice of the assessee where the annual value will be taken as nil)
c. Deemed let-out properties, i.e. properties in addition to the above, not actually let out, where income would be calculated on a notional basis.

In either case, the first thing to do is to arrive at the annual value of the house property.

The annual value of a self-occupied property is nil.

The annual value of a let-out property is the higher of

a) Rent received
b) Municipal rateable value
c) Fair rental value

The annual value of a deemed let-out property is the higher of

a) Municipal rateable value
b) Fair rental value

From the annual value a deduction for municipal taxes paid is to be made. (This deduction is not available to a self-occupied house)

The resultant figure is called Net Annual Value or NAV.

From the NAV, two further deductions are permitted:

1) 30 per cent of NAV as standard deduction (assumed to have been spent on repairs, maintenance and other expenses)
2) Interest on loan taken for purchase, construction, repairs, etc., of the house property (subject to a specified limit in case of self-occupied and deemed let-out house and the actual interest in case of let-out properties)

This will give you the NET INCOME FROM HOUSE PROPERTY

Calculation of income from house property

	Self-occupied Property	Let-out property	Deemed let-out property
Annual value	✗	Higher of Rent received Municipal value or Fair rental value	Higher of Municipal value or Fair rental value
Municipal taxes paid	Not permitted	Permitted	Permitted
(NAV)	✗	✓	✓
Standard Deduction	✗	30% of NAV	30% of NAV
Interest on loan	Subject to a limit	Actual interest paid	Subject to a limit
Net income from house property	✓ (-ve income)	✓	✓

3. Profits and gains of business or profession

This being a book on personal finance, I will not be discussing how to arrive at income from business. Suffice it to say that every business organization prepares a P&L account revealing the profit which has been arrived at after deducting the expenses from the income. This figure, with some adjustments (for disallowable expenses, etc.) is the **NET INCOME FROM BUSINESS.**

4. Capital gains

Capital gain is a gain arising on transfer of a capital asset.

Capital gain is a gain arising on transfer of a capital asset.
In order to be considered as capital gain two ingredients are essential, viz. there should be a 'transfer' and the transfer should be of a 'capital asset'.

Capital asset

Capital asset includes property of any kind whether movable (eg. shares) or immovable (eg. land), tangible or intangible. However certain assets have been excluded from the definition of capital assets for the purpose of capital gain tax. Amongst these are:

a. Any stock-in-trade, consumable stores or raw materials held for the purpose of business or profession (for eg. jewellery held by say a housewife as a piece of ornament will be a capital asset and a gain on sale will be charged to tax as capital gain. Jewellery held by a jeweller would not be a capital asset but stock-in-trade and hence the gain on sale would be taxed business gain)

b. Personal effects of the assessee, that is to say, movable property including wearing apparel and furniture held for his personal use or for the use of any member of his family dependent upon him (from the assessment year 1973–74, jewellery is treated as a capital asset, even though it is meant for personal use of the assessee).

Transfer

Please note that capital gain arises on transfer of a capital asset. The word used is 'transfer' and not 'sale'. Selling an asset is one mode of transfer. However transfer, in relation to a capital asset, includes the exchange or relinquishment of the asset or the extinguishment of any right therein or the compulsory acquisition thereof under any law, etc.

Transfer of movable property is complete on delivery. Transfer of immovable property is normally complete on delivery and when the conveyance is registered. This provision was amended to state that transfer in case of immovable property includes possession of immovable property given without the registration of a conveyance deed.

Types of capital asset

There are two types of capital assets: long-term and short-term. A short term capital asset usually means capital held for not more than thirty-six months immediately prior to its date of transfer. This period has now been reduced to twenty-four months in the case of immovable property being land, building, and house property. An asset other than a short term capital asset is regarded as a long term capital asset.

However shares in a company and units of mutual funds are treated as long-term capital assets if they are held for a period of more than one year.

Consequently, when a long-term capital asset is sold, the gain or loss is called a long-term capital gain or loss and when a short-term capital asset is sold the gain or loss is called a short-term capital gain or loss.

Computation of short-term capital gains

To arrive at short-term capital gains for an asset sold:

Step 1: Take the sale value (This is called the **Gross Consideration**)

Step 2: Deduct the costs incurred in the process of transfer
This will give you the **Net Consideration**

Step 3: From the Net Consideration deduct

a. The cost of acquisition of the asset and
b. The cost of improvement incurred on the asset

The resultant figure is the Short-Term Capital Gain

How to compute **Short-Term** Capital Gains

Gross Consideration (received or accruing on transfer)
Less: Cost of Transfer = Net Consideration
Less: Cost of Acquisition
Less: Cost of Improvement
= Short-Term Capital Gains

Computation of Long-Term Capital Gains

To arrive at long-term capital gains for an asset sold, steps 1 and 2 are the same

Step 1: Take the sale value (called the **Gross Consideration)**

Step 2: Deduct the costs incurred in the process of transfer

This will give you the **Net Consideration**

Step 3: From the Net Consideration

a. Instead of the cost of acquisition, **the indexed cost of acquisition, can be deducted.**
(Indexed cost of acquisition is arrived at after adjusting the cost for inflation by applying the cost inflation index).

b. Similarly the **Indexed Cost of Improvement** can also be deducted.

Cost Inflation Index

Financial Year	INDEX	Financial Year	INDEX	Financial Year	INDEX
1981–82	100	1993–94	244	2005–06	497
1982–83	109	1994–95	259	2006–07	519
1983–84	116	1995–96	281	2007–08	551
1984–85	125	1996–97	305	2008–09	582
1985–86	133	1997–98	331	2009–10	632
1986–87	140	1998–99	351	2010–11	711
1987–88	150	1999–00	389	2011–12	785
1988–89	161	2000–01	406	2012–13	852
1989–90	172	2001–02	426	2013–14	939
1990–91	182	2002–03	447	2014–15	1024
1991–92	199	2003–04	463	2015–16	1081
1992–93	223	2004–05	480	2016–17	1125

The New Cost Inflation Index Wef 2017

Financial Year	INDEX	Financial Year	INDEX
2001–02	100	2010–11	167
2002–03	105	2011–12	184
2003–04	109	2012–13	200
2004–05	113	2013–14	220
2005–06	117	2014–15	240
2006–07	122	2015–16	254
2007–08	129	2016–17	264
2008–09	137	2017–18	272
2009–10	148	2018–19	280

This will give you the Long-Term Capital Gain.

How to compute **Long-Term** Capital Gains

Gross Consideration
Less: Cost of Transfer = **Net Consideration**
Less: Indexed Cost of Acquisition
Less: Indexed Cost of Improvement
= Long-Term Capital Gains

Do keep in mind, this is not a comprehensive discussion on how to calculate capital gains. There are many more dimensions and other factors to be taken into account. For actual calculation I would urge you to take the help of a chartered accountant or your tax consultant.

Taxation of short-term capital gains

Short-term capital gains are taxed as normal income (except short-term capital gains on transfer of shares or units of mutual funds which are taxed at a special rate). In other words these gains are added to income from whatever other sources the person may have. Very little opportunity is available to reduce or avoid the tax liability. As a result a person who earns short-term capital gains lands up paying a substantial portion of the gains as tax.

Taxation of long-term capital gains

Long-term capital gains on the other hand are subject to a number of deductions and exemptions, and one who consciously takes advantage of these deductions will find that all or a substantial portion of the tax liability can be avoided.

Some of these exemptions and deductions are available under sections 54, 54EC, and 54F.

Section 54: Capital gain on transfer of house property
This section provides for exemption of capital gains arising from transfer of house property which is held for a minimum period of three years.

The exemption is available if the capital gain component is used to purchase one residential house in India either one year before the date of transfer of the original asset or it may be purchased within two years after the date. The time available is three years after the transfer if a house is constructed.

The capital gain will be fully exempt if the entire capital gain or more is so invested. And if it is partially invested, the exemption will be confined to the amount invested and the balance will be taxed at a specified special rate applicable to long-term capital gains.

The new house purchased cannot be sold for three years from the date of purchase/construction. If it is sold, the difference between the sale price and the cost of the new house as reduced by the amount of capital gain exempted will be chargeable as short-term capital gain and treated as income of the year in which the new asset is sold.

Section 54EC: Capital gains on transfer of long term capital asset

Exemption under this section is available to capital gain from transfer of any long-term capital asset (from 2018–19 only applicable on transfer of land or building or both) provided the whole or a part of the capital gains is invested in the purchase of certain specified assets.

The investment is to be made within six months after the transfer of the asset and is at present subject to an upper limit.

So the entire amount of capital gain can be exempted if the capital gain is less than the specified limit, or it can be partially exempted to the extent of the limit.

Section 54F: Capital gains on transfer of a long-term capital asset other than house property

Exemption under Section 54F is available to capital gains arising from any long-term capital asset other than a house property.

This exemption is available if the net consideration (and not the capital gains) is used to purchase within one year before or two years after the date of transfer or to construct within three years one residential house in India.

This exemption is subject to the condition that the person should not own more than one residential house (other than the new house) on the date of transfer of the original asset. Further he should also not purchase within a period of one year or construct within a period of three years any residential house (other than the new house) after such date.

If the entire capital gain is invested, the amount will be wholly exempted. And if it is partially invested then only proportionate capital gain will be exempted.

The new house has to be retained for at least three years from the date of purchase or construction. And the person should also not purchase another house for at least two years or construct any residential house for a period of three years from the date of transfer of the original asset.

Long-term capital gains on the assets sold after adjusting for exemptions along with the short term capital gains will give you the **NET INCOME FROM CAPITAL GAINS.**

5. Income from other sources

Income which has not so far been classified into the previous four heads of income is chargeable under the head Income from Other Sources.
Items under this head include income from interest, dividends, winnings from lotteries, horse races, card games, etc.

After deducting 'reasonable expenses' incurred to earn these incomes, the balance is the **NET INCOME FROM OTHER SOURCES.**

We have now completed STEP I. We have computed the NET INCOME from the various heads.
Now we move on to Step II.

STEP II: Add the NET INCOMES to arrive at the GROSS TOTAL INCOME.

Addition of all the NET INCOMES does not give you the net total income, but is again called the GROSS TOTAL INCOME.

The word 'gross' indicates that this is not yet the taxable income, and some deductions can still be claimed.

So, we now proceed to Step III.

STEP III: Claim deductions available under Chapter VIA or Section 80 of the Income Tax Act and arrive at the TOTAL INCOME

Chapter VIA of the Income Tax Act contains Section 80. This may sound like just one section but is very vast in scope. It includes numerous sub-sections, starting from 80C, 80CCC, 80 CCD and goes up to 80U.

All these sub-sections prescribe deductions available from gross total income, the effect of which is to reduce the taxable income.

Let me tell you about a few of the popular sub-sections.

Section 80C: This section provides for deduction in respect of certain investments made, subject to an upper limit.

The items that qualify for deduction under this section include life insurance premium paid, contribution to employees' provident fund account, purchase of National Savings Certificates, contribution to PPF accounts, payment of children's school fees, repayment of housing loan instalments, subscription to certain approved equity shares or debentures, making fixed deposits in banks for a minimum period of five years, investing in equity linked savings schemes of mutual funds, purchase of ULIPs and a few more items.

Section 80D: Deduction is permitted under Section 80D for health insurance premia paid, subject to limits.

Section 80G: This section allows deduction for donations made to certain types of charitable and other institutions and funds.

Section 80TTA: Interest on deposits in savings accounts up to a certain limit is exempt under Section 80TTA.

Section 80TTB: Interest on deposits in savings accounts earned by senior citizens up to a substantially higher limit as compared to that under Section 80TTA is permitted under Section 80TTB.

The gross total income arrived at as per Step II reduced by the deductions under Chapter VIA as per Step III, give you the total income, which is also the taxable income.

We now move on to Step IV.

STEP IV: **Arrive at the tax liability**

The total income will now be divided into two parts: one to be taxed at special rates and the other at normal rates which would be as per the prescribed slabs.

We can now move to the last step.

STEP V: **Compare the tax liability with the pre-assessment taxes paid (by way of TDS and Advance Tax).**

The tax worked out as per Step IV, has hopefully already been paid. Some tax probably has been deducted at source and the law also expects you to pay advance tax. The TDS and advance tax together are called the pre-assessment taxes.

If, on comparing the tax payable with the pre-assessment taxes paid, you find that the tax paid is more than the tax due, you can claim a refund while filing the income tax return.

And in case the tax already paid falls short of the tax payable, you will have to pay the difference by way of self-assessment tax before filing the income tax return.

Please note: The discussion on income tax matters in this chapter is meant to provide an overall idea to the readers of the tax implication of many of their decisions and should not be construed as the professional advice or opinion of the author. The information provided is not comprehensive but illustrative. Also keep in mind that tax laws are subject to frequent amendments and it is possible that several of the tax provisions cited here may have changed by the time you are reading this. You are advised to consult a chartered accountant or tax consultant before putting into practice any suggestion made here.

'An investment in knowledge always pays the best interest.'

Benjamin Franklin

Chapter 10

Investments Providing Tax Relief

Section 80C of the Income Tax Act specifies several investments including provident fund, pension schemes, life insurance and equity linked savings scheme to debt instruments and products such as National Savings Certificates (NSC), PPF, tax-saving fixed deposits with banks or the post office etc., which provide tax relief. Investment in these avenues, up to a maximum of Rs 1.5 lakh per annum is currently deductible from gross total income.

Each avenue has its own pros and cons. Some like equity linked savings schemes have a shorter lock-in of three years, but carry relatively higher risk, while others come with a longer lock-in period (till age fifty-five in case of employees' provident fund and fifteen years for PPF), but are safe investments. Returns also vary from low (as in the case of insurance) to moderate (debt-oriented schemes like NSC and PPF) to reasonably high (ELSS).

Both NSC and tax-saving fixed deposits have a lock-in period of five years. Those looking for short-term debt investments which offer Section 80C tax benefits and also a high degree of safety would choose between these two.

Let us examine in detail a few of these tax saving investments.

A. Public Provident Fund

Open a PPF account early and there is no need to do any other retirement planning

Investing in PPF is an excellent way of saving, which also gives a tax deduction. Even if one does not get any tax advantage by virtue of the fact that the maximum deduction available under Section 80C is being exhausted through some other investments made, it still makes ample sense to invest in PPF.

Let me explain why.

Let's take a look at the features of this account and its advantages.

The amount of deposit and the period of the account
PPF is a fifteen years account. One is obliged to deposit a minimum of Rs 500 each year, and it is possible to deposit up to a maximum of Rs 150,000 as per rules in force currently.

Tax deduction, rate of interest and other benefits
The amount invested in a PPF account is eligible for a deduction under Section 80C of the Income Tax Act, subject to the conditions of the section.

The PPF account earns interest which is compounded annually.

The entire interest earned is exempt from income tax under Section 10 of the Income Tax Act, without any limits.

The entire balance in a PPF account is exempt from wealth tax. Earlier this exemption was not available to other deposits, but now even other investments and bank balances are exempt from wealth tax.

An account for a rainy day

The amount saved in a PPF account is actually saving for a rainy day. God forbid, if bad days fall upon someone and debts pile up, probably all the assets of the person can get attached. However, no court of law in India has the power to order attachment of the balance in a PPF account and hence the debtors cannot access one's PPF account to claim the dues. However, it does not apply to the income tax authorities and so the amount standing to the credit of a depositor in the PPF account is liable to attachment under any order of income tax authorities with respect to debt or liability incurred by the person.

> **No court of law in India has the power to order attachment of the balance in a PPF account**

The tenure

The fifteen years tenure was responsible for this investment not to become very popular initially since many taxpayers found it more attractive to invest in National Savings Certificates which had a far shorter maturity period. But this was out of sheer ignorance about the various advantages of PPF.

The period of fifteen years is actually nothing to get concerned about, and in fact, once a person gets acquainted with its advantages s/he actually starts wishing that the account was of a longer duration. For this purpose it is permitted, on maturity, to extend the account indefinitely in blocks of five years.

Besides, the PPF scheme follows the fiscal year (that is the period April 1 to March 31) as its accounting year. Even if you open the account on March 31, on the very next day one year is over and only fourteen years will be left.

For those of you who have not been investing in PPF and instead choose something like National Savings Certificate because of the shorter duration of maturity, I think investing in PPF can be of even shorter duration than any other investment.

How is that possible?

You open this account and for the first ten to twelve years deposit only the bare minimum amount that is required to keep the account alive. Now in the thirteenth year invest the maximum permissible amount. You will get all the advantages of investing in a PPF account like tax deduction, a pretty decent interest, tax exemption on the interest, etc., and will also get your money back in three years. The amount deposited in the fourteenth year will come back in two years and the sum deposited in the fifteenth year will come back in one year. I think it is worth opening the account just to take advantage of the fifteenth year of deposit. But I don't suggest you do this. I think you should deposit a substantial amount each year and the real advantage of this account can be reaped if you do not withdraw the amount and let it accumulate over a number of years.

The amount deposited in the account can be different each year. Since the minimum amount to be deposited is Rs 500, in a particular year if one does not have sufficient disposable surplus, one needs to only deposit this minimum sum to keep the account alive. In fact if one finds even Rs 500 to be high, one can deposit Rs 42 each month since the account allows up to twelve deposits each year, one per month.

And even if Rs 42 per month pinches, I suggest don't deposit anything. But still open this account. What will happen if you do not deposit any money? The account will lapse. Let it lapse. If a few years later you realize the advantages of having a PPF account and if you open an account then you will have to wait another fifteen years for the account to mature. But if you open the account now and it lapses, you can revive the account by depositing Rs 500 for each year that you did not pay along with a penalty of Rs 50 for each year of default and the account gets revived.

And what if one is in dire need of money before the fifteen-year tenure of the account is over? This is also nothing to worry about since the account allows a loan to be taken after the third year and there is also a withdrawal facility after the sixth year (as explained below).

Besides it is possible to prematurely close the account after five years. As per an amendment proposed to amend the rules of the account, investors will be allowed to withdraw their money from a PPF account in case of exigencies, such as medical emergencies or higher education needs.

Loan and withdrawal facility

Loan is admissible from the third year. The loan amount is limited to 25 per cent of the balance at the end of two preceding years. A fresh loan is not allowed when previous loan or interest thereof is outstanding. Interest is charged at the rate of 1 per cent if repaid within thirty-six months and at 6 per cent on the outstanding loan after thirty-six months.

Withdrawal is permissible every year from the seventh financial year since the year of opening, limited to one per year.

Amount of withdrawal is limited to 50 per cent of the balance at the end of the fourth preceding year or 50 per cent of the balance at the end of the immediate preceding year, whichever is less. 'Balance at the end of the preceding year' means the immediately preceding March 31.
Let me illustrate the withdrawal facility assuming you are depositing Rs 1,50,000 each year. *I am going to ignore interest for the purpose of this calculation and will leave it to your imagination how much more attractive it will become if you take that into account too.*

For the first six years withdrawal is not permitted. In the seventh year you can withdraw either 50 per cent of Rs 9,00,000 (that is the balance at the end of the immediately preceding year) or 50 per cent of Rs 4,50,000 (balance at the

Table 1

YEAR	Opening Balance	Deposit	Withdrawal	Closing Balance
1	0	1,50,000	0	1,50,000
2	1,50,000	1,50,000	0	3,00,000
3	3,00,000	1,50,000	0	4,50,000
4	4,50,000	1,50,000	0	6,00,000
5	6,00,000	1,50,000	0	7,50,000
6	7,50,000	1,50,000	0	9,00,000
7	9,00,000	1,50,000	2,25,000	8,25,000
8	8,25,000	1,50,000	3,00,000	6,75,000
9	6,75,000	1,50,000	3,37,500	4,87,500
10	4,87,500	1,50,000	2,43,750	3,93,750
11	3,93,750	1,50,000	1,96,875	3,46,875
12	3,46,875	1,50,000	1,73,438	3,23,438
13	3,23,438	1,50,000	1,61,719	3,11,719
14	3,11,719	1,50,000	1,55,859	3,05,859
15	3,05,859	1,50,000	1,52,930	3,02,930

end of the fourth preceding year), whichever is lower. So the maximum permissible withdrawal would be Rs 2,25,000. In the eighth year the withdrawal would be 50 per cent of the lower of Rs 8,25,000 or Rs 6,00,000 and so on.

Now watch table 1 carefully. Do you see anything particularly attractive about it?

How much have you deposited each year? And how much is the amount of withdrawal each year after the sixth? The amount withdrawn is more than the amount deposited each year right up to the fifteenth year. In other words the out of pocket investment is nil. And so far, I have ignored interest. If you take into account the interest, the amount that you are eligible to withdraw would be substantially more than what I have illustrated. Which means that all one has to do after the sixth year is to go to the bank, withdraw the amount permissible, deposit out of the same amount Rs 1,50,000, actually bring money home, and enjoy an income tax deduction. And this can be done right up to the maturity of the account.

But I would not recommend that you do this. By all means do it if you are in need of money. But if that is not the case, then I would rather you make a fresh investment in the account each year. That is the only way you can take maximum benefit of the PPF account.

The rate of interest on the PPF account has lately been an average of 8 per cent (+/- 0.75 per cent).

Imagine that someone opens a PPF account, deposits Rs 1,50,000 each year, and renews the account every five years after the initial fifteen years.

Table 2	
Yearly Deposit	Interest Rate
150000	8.0 per cent

Year	Op Bal	Deposit	Interest	Cl Balance
1	0	1,50,000	12,000	1,62,000
2	1,62,000	1,50,000	24,960	3,36,960
3	3,36,960	1,50,000	38,957	5,25,917
4	5,25,917	1,50,000	54,073	7,29,990
5	7,29,990	1,50,000	70,399	9,50,389
10	20,22,984	1,50,000	1,73,839	23,46,823
15	39,22,818	1,50,000	3,25,825	43,98,643
20	67,14,295	1,50,000	5,49,144	74,13,439
25	1,08,15,891	1,50,000	8,77,271	1,18,43,162
30	1,68,42,482	1,50,000	13,59,399	1,83,51,881
35	2,56,97,521	1,50,000	20,67,802	2,79,15,323
40	3,87,08,478	1,50,000	31,08,678	4,19,67,156
50	8,59,15,523	1,50,000	68,85,242	9,29,50,765
60	18,78,31,994	1,50,000	1,50,38,560	2,03,02,0554

Take a look at table 2 illustrating the interest earned and the closing balance in the account after five, ten, fifteen, twenty, thirty, forty, fifty and sixty years assuming an interest rate of 8 per cent.

At the end of ten years the principal amount deposited is Rs 15 lakh and the closing balance is over Rs 23 lakh. After twenty years Rs 30 lakh is the principal and closing balance over Rs 74 lakh. After thirty and forty years the principal amounts of Rs 45 and 60 lakh, have grown to Rs 118 lakh and Rs 420 lakh respectively. And after fifty and sixty years the principal amounts invested are Rs 75 lakh and Rs 90 lakh and the closing balances have increased to a staggering sums of Rs 9 crore 30 lakh and 20 crore 30 lakh respectively. Do you see the power of compounding in action here?

Which is why it is so important to open this account as early in life as possible, and to keep depositing till one is ready to retire.

Now you can also see why I was against using the amount withdrawn each year to make the deposit. As far as possible deposit a fresh amount and the amount should stay in the PPF account for as long as possible.

One who opens a PPF account at the age of say twenty-five years, can easily deposit in the account for thirty-five years or even more. One of the finest gifts parents can give to their child is a PPF account opened in the child's name soon after birth. The parents can deposit money for the first twenty to twenty-five years of the child's life and thereafter the child starts depositing in the account till the age of say sixty. Can you imagine the amount that would get accumulated?

I have always felt, that if one has systematically deposited money in a PPF account, starting relatively early in life, even if no other retirement planning has been done, this account alone can suffice.

In table 2, at the end of thirty-five years the closing balance is about Rs 2.79 crore and the interest earned in the year is over Rs 20 lakh. And at the end of forty years the balance is Rs 4.20 crore and the interest is over Rs 31 lakh. Imagine a couple, both of whom have a PPF account which at the time of their retirement has been active for thirty-five to forty years, a closing balance of anywhere between Rs 2.79 crore to Rs 4.20 crore, earn interest per annum of, say, anywhere between Rs 20 lakh to Rs 30 lakh each. By the time of retirement, most family responsibilities have been taken care of, the children are settled, the house and the car are already there. To take care of their day to day expenses and more, they need to simply withdraw the interest component between them amounting to about Rs 50 lakh per annum which is tax-free. And the nest egg in the form of the principal amount is safe and intact.
Now I know your immediate reaction is going to be

'What if the laws change?', or 'What if the scheme gets discontinued?' or 'What if the tax exemption is withdrawn?' All I would like to say is, since one doesn't know the future, one can only plan on the basis of what is applicable today. Personally, I have been strongly advocating this account for over twenty years now. And these questions were posed even twenty years ago. Till date the account is still there. It is just the interest rate that has been revised downward (in keeping with a general reduction of interest rates on other deposits too). All other features have actually become more attractive. Earlier a service charge at the rate of 1 per cent was levied on withdrawals. Now there is none. Earlier extension was permitted for five years at a time for merely three times. Now there is no restriction. And of course it would be a pity if, being sceptical, one were to not take advantage of this investment when thirty or forty years later in all its glory, the account could still be around.

B. National Savings Certificates

A National Savings Certificate, popularly known as NSC, is a savings bond.

The inception of the NSC can be traced back to the 1950s when the government issued savings certificates in order to raise money to help fund the development of a new and independent India. They are issued by the post office and can be taken from any branch of the Indian postal service. There are two types of NSC certificates that are available at present: NSC Issues VIII and IX.

1. NSC Issue VIII was intended to provide an investment avenue for those looking for safe instruments to invest in and also avail tax benefits at the same time. These certificates come with a shorter maturity of five years, in denominations ranging from Rs 100 to Rs 10,000 but earn a lower interest rate compared to Issue IX.

2. NSC Issue IX certificates also come in denominations ranging from Rs 100 to Rs 10,000 and with an interest that is slightly higher than that offered for Issue VIII and with a maturity period of ten years.

Both series VIII and IX certificates can be pledged to banks as collateral for availing loans.

Investment in NSCs enjoys tax benefit under Section 80C of the Income Tax Act.

The interest earned is to be added to the income of the year and is subject to tax.

However, the interest earned on these bonds annually is not physically paid out, but gets accumulated and is paid together with the principal sum on maturity. Since the amount of interest is not paid but remains with the post office, it is treated as a deemed re-investment in NSC and also becomes eligible for deduction under Section 80C.

In other words, a person investing in this bond enjoys an income tax deduction in the year of purchase for the amount invested and also gets a deduction on the interest earned each year (except the last year's interest, which is not reinvested but paid back to the depositor).

Features

- These certificates can be taken by individuals singly as well as in a joint investment.
- Unlike in the case of PPF, there is no limit on the amount that a person can invest in an NSC.
- These bonds can be purchased by individuals and not companies, trusts, or Hindu Unified Families.
- NSCs range in denominations from Rs 100 to Rs 10,000.
- Investments cannot be withdrawn prematurely unless the case involves the death of the primary holders.
- Nomination facilities are also provided under both Issue VIII and Issue IX.

Benefits

- Investments made in an NSC are eligible for deduction under Section 80C of the Income Tax Act.
- The interest earned can be virtually tax-free except for the interest that is earned in the last year.

- There is no upper limit on the amount that can be invested in these certificates.
- If the certificates are lost or damaged, duplicates can be arranged.
- The interest earned is compounded and reinvested in the scheme by default which means that without purchasing extra certificates, you can increase the invested amount.
- Post-maturity, the amount received can be reinvested in the scheme by purchasing fresh certificates equal to the maturity amount.
- The certificates can also be taken on behalf of a minor.
- The investment can be used to secure loans.

No TDS deduction on interest in NSC

The interest accrued in the NSC does not attract TDS, which is not the case with a fixed deposit kept in a bank.

If an FD and NSC are invested in with the same principal amount, the NSC will provide a higher maturity amount at the end of the maturity period. Plus, no TDS will be deducted during the five years, so there is no hassle of filing income tax returns. Hence, NSC is proved to have an edge over FDs.

Premature withdrawals

NSC investment comes with a lock-in period that is equal to the maturity of the certificates. The amount can be withdrawn prematurely if:

- The holder of the NSC passes away.
- The holder of the certificate has forfeited the bonds through a pledge.
- A court of law has ordered that the NSC be paid prematurely.

C. National Pension Scheme

National Pension Scheme (NPS) is a government-sponsored pension scheme which was initially launched for government employees. In 2009, it was opened to all Indian citizens between eighteen and sixty years.

Contributions can be made regularly in a pension account during the subscribers' working life. It is permitted to withdraw a part of the corpus in a lump sum and the remaining corpus can be used to buy an annuity to secure a regular income after retirement.

What is an annuity?

An annuity provides a regular income, which could be monthly, quarterly or annually, at a specified rate for a specified period chosen by the subscriber. In NPS, a subscriber must use at least 40 per cent of the corpus to buy an annuity. This can be done by paying the amount to an annuity service provider (ASP) and choosing an annuity option to ensure a regular income after retirement.

How to open the account?

NPS accounts are opened with entities known as points of presence (POP). Most banks, both private and public sector, are enrolled as POPs. Several financial institutions also act as POPs. The authorized branches of a POP, called point of presence-service providers (POP-SPs), act as collection points.

Only one NPS account can be opened by one individual and the minimum contribution required is Rs 1,000 per financial year.

Tax benefits

In case the contributor is an employee, the payer's own contribution is eligible for a tax deduction—up to 10 per cent of the salary (basic plus DA)—under Section 80CCD(1) of the Income Tax Act within the overall ceiling of Rs 1.5 lakh allowed under Section 80C and Section 80CCE.

The employer's contribution to NPS is exempted under Section 80CCD(2).

Moreover, individuals can claim an additional deduction of up to Rs 50,000 under Section 80CCD(1B), which is in addition to Rs 1.5 lakh permitted under Section 80C. In case of a self-employed person, 10 per cent of the gross income can be contributed under Section 80CCD(1) in NPS.

Withdrawal facility

NPS, being a pension product, the contributor is expected to stay invested until retirement. At age sixty, at least 40 per cent of the corpus must be used to buy an annuity income from the Pension Fund Regulatory and Development Authority (PFRDA)-listed insurance company. Another 40 per cent of the corpus may be withdrawn, which is tax-free. The remaining 20 per cent of the corpus could either be withdrawn, in which case it will be taxed as per the income tax slab applicable to the recipient, or it can be used to buy further annuity.

One can, if one so chooses, defer the withdrawal of the lump sum amount till age seventy.

And in case one wishes to opt out of the scheme before attaining age sixty, just about 20 per cent of the accumulated corpus can be withdrawn and 80 per cent must be used to purchase an annuity.

In the event of the death of the subscriber, the entire accumulated amount would be paid to the nominee/legal heir of the subscriber.

D. Equity Linked Savings Schemes (ELSS)

Popularly known as ELSS, equity linked savings schemes are among the better schemes offered by mutual funds.

Tax deduction

Investment in ELSS attracts tax deduction under Section 80C (subject to limits). These are close-ended investment options and come with a three year lock-in period, which is the shortest among all other investment options that provide tax relief. Consequently, investment in ELSS provides better liquidity compared to other options like bank fixed deposits, NSC, PPF and NPS, all of which have lock-in periods of five years or more.

Investment in ELSS can be made using both SIP as well as lump sum investment options.

Maximum tax exemption limit

Section 80C is an extensive section which includes numerous investment avenues, like Employees Provident Fund (EPF) and life insurance policy, that are eligible for tax deduction. The maximum tax exemption limit available under Section 80C is Rs 1.5 lakh. If you have already claimed some of the exemption via other investments, then your entire investment in ELSS may not be available for deduction. Thus, before finalizing your investment amount do remember to perform some basic calculations to take an informed decision.

Exposure to equity

The funds invest the money collected in equities and equity-related securities and thereby provide higher returns.

For those who wish to invest in equities but don't know how to go about it, a good way to begin is through investing in ELSS. Along with professional fund management, you get the benefit of a well-diversified portfolio at a nominal initial investment.

Higher risk

Since the fund invests predominantly in equity stocks of companies, the risk of fluctuation in Net Asset Value (NAV) is also higher.
To mitigate the risk one should try and stay invested for a longer duration in excess of five years, even though the lock-in period is three years.

Expectation of maximum returns

As compared to other asset classes, equity funds have been found to give above average returns in the long run. However, there are no guaranteed returns. The performance of the fund may vary across different time horizons. Only if you stay invested for a longer investment period can you hope for higher returns.

Conclusion

Taking into account the tax deductibility of this investment, the shorter lock-in period compared to other similar investments, and the higher returns due to exposure to equity, this investment appears to be an attractive addition to one's personal finance portfolio.

E. Fixed Deposit

Section 80C also provides for deduction for investing in certain fixed deposits.

Tax-saving fixed deposits are like regular fixed deposits but come with a lock-in period of five years. This account can be opened by resident Indian individuals and Hindu Undivided Families.

The rate of interest varies across banks and ranges between 5.5 per cent and 7.75 per cent.

The interest earned on these deposits is taxable.

Features

Key features of this type of account are:
Tax-saving fixed deposits have a fixed maturity of five years.

- The minimum investment must be Rs 100. Further investments can be made in multiples of Rs 100 only.
- The maximum limit of investments is capped at Rs 1.5 lakh, (revised from the earlier limit of Rs 1 lakh).
- It provides tax deductions on amount invested up to Rs 1.5 lakh per year.

- Premature withdrawal is not permitted.
- Only a one-time lump sum deposit is permitted.
- Provides flexibility in the amount to be invested.
- Loans cannot be availed against tax saver fixed deposit accounts.
- Tax is deducted at source on income earned through interests from this account. TDS is charged at 10 per cent p.a. if the account holder has submitted his/her PAN details. Else TDS will be charged at 20 per cent p.a.
- The facility is available throughout the year unlike tax free bonds issued by the government which are offered from time to time.
- Interest is paid out on a monthly or quarterly basis.
- Special rates are offered for senior citizens as per the provider.
- Secure investments for the medium term.

Tax-saving fixed deposits may not generate returns as high as some other tax saving investments such as mutual funds, but provide a peace of mind due to the assurance of safety, and the depositor gets assured pay-outs at regular intervals.

F. Unit Linked Insurance Plan

ULIP is a product offered by insurance companies that gives investors both insurance and investment under a single integrated plan.
It is a combination of insurance and an investment vehicle. The policyholder can pay a monthly or annual premium, a small portion of which goes towards life insurance premium and the balance is invested just like a mutual fund in equity and debt instruments.

The policyholder continues to invest through the term of the policy, which could be five, ten or fifteen years and accumulates the units. Investors have the option to invest in equity or debt.
Each policyholder has the option to select a personalized investment mix based on individual needs and risk appetite. A conservative investor can go for the debt

option, while an aggressive one can opt for the equity oriented fund which is also called a growth option.

Like mutual funds, each policyholder's ULIP holds a certain number of fund units, each of which has a NAV that is declared on a daily basis which varies from one ULIP to another based on market conditions and fund performance.

A ULIP is typically opened by an investor seeking to provide coverage for beneficiaries. The investor pays premiums with the intention of the plan's sum assured to be paid out at a certain time frame for a specific beneficiary who would receive payments following the owner's death. Plans can include varying provisions for triggering payments.

A unit linked insurance plan's investment options are structured similar to a mutual fund. Different ULIPs offer different qualified investments.
Investors can buy shares in a single strategy or diversify their investments across multiple market-linked ULIP funds.

ULIPs require a premium that varies with the terms of each ULIP. An initial lump sum is typically required along with periodical premium payments. The premiums are proportionally invested towards specified coverage and in the designated investments.

Investors can make changes to their fund preferences throughout the duration of their investment. The funds offer transferring flexibility. Numerous investment options are also available including stock funds, bond funds and diversified funds.

Personally, I have always been against combining insurance and investment. While investing, one should choose a pure investment. Similarly while choosing an insurance plan, the only consideration should be coverage. Any attempt at combining the two results in a sub-standard investment and a less than optimum insurance plan.

To sum it up

For most people, investment in an ELSS scheme would be attractive on account of the potential for higher returns, coupled with tax-deductibility of the sum invested and a short lock-in period.

Salary-earners usually have a certain amount that gets invested through PF deductions. For the difference between the maximum permissible amount under Section 80C and the PF contribution, equity would be advisable. ELSSs enjoy the unique feature of being the only tax-saving investment for the purpose of Section 80C that also provides the benefit of equity returns.

Investment	Returns	Lock-in-Period	Tax on Returns
5-Year Bank Fixed Desposit	6% to 7%	5 years	Yes
Public Providend Fund (PPF)	7% to 8%	15 years	No
National Savings Certificate	7% to 8%	5 years	Yes
National Pension System (NPS)	8% to 10%	Till Retirement	Partially taxable
ELSS Funds	15% to 18%	3 Years	Partially taxable

Of course, investments made in ULIPs and the NPS also give equity-linked returns, but ULIPs have a longer lock-in period of five years coupled with high costs and poor transparency while the NPS is a retirement solution rather than a savings one, having only partial exposure to equity and a very long lock-in period that effectively extends till retirement age.

'The safest way to double your money is to fold it over twice and put it in your pocket'.

Kim Hubbard

Chapter

11

Investing in Real Estate Investment Trusts (REITs)

What is a REIT?

A Real Estate Investment Trust, or REIT, is an investment vehicle that owns, operates and manages a portfolio of income-producing real estate. These are usually commercial properties like residential and office buildings, warehouses, hospitals, shopping malls and hotels that generate rental income. REIT, in a way, is a mutual fund for real estate assets, to provide investors a chance to earn all types regular income streams, diversification and long-term capital appreciation.

Creation

REITs were created in the United States in 1960 when the Cigar Excise Tax Extension of 1960 was passed. The law was enacted to give all investors the opportunity to invest in large-scale, diversified portfolios of income-producing real estate through the purchase and sale of liquid securities.

Since then, more than thirty countries around the world have established REIT regimes.

REITs have been popular in Asia, chiefly Singapore and Hong Kong, but are relatively new in India.

REITs in India

In India, the Real Estate Investment Trusts were introduced by the SEBI in 2007. The proposal was later on rejected. In September, 2013, SEBI came out with revised regulations for REITs, which were approved on 26 September 2014.

REITs have many advantages for interested investors. It provides a regular income stream along with reduced portfolio volatility and dividends and wealth accumulation. As a result of it being a listed entity, it is bought and sold with ease providing great liquidity. It is a natural hedge against inflation as returns have been seen to consistently outpace consumer price inflation.

There are primarily two types of REITs: equity and mortgage. Real Estate Investment Trusts are extremely beneficial for the development of an economy as they allow dormant investable funds to be channelled into infrastructure projects such as apartment complexes, hospitals, schools and the likes.

The main target of REITs will be shopping malls, hotels, offices, nursing homes, etc. At present, in India, REITs will not be allowed to buy residential buildings.

Why is it important?

The Indian real estate sector has been facing a liquidity crunch on account of unsold inventory and low demand. REITs can help cash-strapped developers to monetise their existing property. Indian investors don't have too many regular income options. SEBI requires REITs to distribute a minimum 90 per cent of their income earned to investors on a half-yearly basis. Similarly, 90 per cent of the sale proceeds too are to be paid out to unit holders unless the amount is reinvested in another property. Thus, you get to receive regular income and also get to benefit from price appreciation, thereby boosting your returns. In the real estate sector, both rent and capital appreciation from property depend on the location, infrastructure and industrial development around that area. REITs juggle these risks through a diversified portfolio.

REITs typically pay out all of their taxable income as dividends to shareholders.

SEBI requires Indian REITs to be listed on exchanges and to make an initial public offer to raise money.

Just like in the case of mutual funds, REITs are subject to a three-tier structure—the sponsor who is responsible for setting up the REIT, the fund management company which is responsible for selecting and operating the properties, and the trustee who ensures that the money is managed in the interest of unit-holders.

You can invest in REITs in primary and secondary markets and exit any time you want. But they will have a minimum investment requirement of Rs 2 lakh. Also, the minimum offer size of an REIT is Rs 250 crore.

Though countries such as the US and Singapore have seen REITs providing good returns, in India, issues such as lower rental yields and an illiquid and opaque property market have so far discouraged REITs.

In my opinion, investing through REITs is a good way to own a piece of the real estate pie without having to invest the huge amounts that such investments normally require if one were to go it alone.

'I don't know what the seven wonders of the world are, but I do know the eighth—compound interest.'

Baron Rothschild
of Tring in the
County of Hertford

Chapter 12

Cryptocurrencies: To Invest or Not to Invest

Bitcoin

Bitcoin was the first cryptocoin currency to have been created.

Bitcoin was invented in 2009 by an unknown person or group of people—cryptocurrencies are designed for maximum anonymity—under the name Satoshi Nakamoto, who has since disappeared.

Bitcoins are created as a reward for a process known as mining. They can be exchanged for other currencies, products and services.

Several hundred thousand merchants and vendors accept bitcoin as payment.

Since 2009, numerous other cryptocurrencies have been created.

These other currencies are collectively called altcoins, or alternative coins.

Why are bitcoins so controversial?

This is because they take the power of making money away from the central banks and give it to the general public.

Governments cannot freeze bitcoin accounts nor can taxmen examine them.

Middlemen banks are not needed for bitcoins to move.

From 2011 to 2013, criminal traders bought bitcoins in batches of millions of dollars to escape the notice of law enforcement agencies.

Blockchain

A blockchain is a continuously growing list of records, called blocks, which are linked and secured using cryptography.

It is decentralized and distributed. A public digital ledger is used to record transactions across many computers so that the record cannot be altered retroactively without the alteration of all subsequent blocks and the collusion of the network.

A distributed or shared ledger is a consensus of replicated, shared and synchronized digital data geographically spread across multiple sites, countries, or institutions. There is no central administrator or centralised data storage.

Each block typically contains a cryptographic hash of the previous block, a timestamp and transaction data.

A blockchain is inherently resistant to modification of the data.

For use as a distributed ledger, a blockchain is typically managed by a peer-to-peer network collectively adhering to a protocol for validating new blocks. Once recorded, the data in any given block cannot be altered.

Mining

In cryptocurrency networks, mining is a validation of transactions. For this effort, successful miners obtain new cryptocurrency as a reward. The reward decreases transaction fees by creating a complementary incentive to contribute to the processing power of the network.

Wallets

A cryptocurrency wallet stores the public and private 'keys' or 'addresses' which can be used to receive or spend the cryptocurrency. With the private key, it is possible to write in the public ledger, effectively spending the associated cryptocurrency. With the public key, it is possible for others to send currency to the wallet.

Legality

The legal status of cryptocurrencies varies substantially from country to country and is still undefined or changing in many of them.

While some countries like the US and Finland have explicitly allowed their use and trade, others like Iceland and Vietnam have banned or restricted it.

The coming months and years will hopefully provide greater clarity of the stance taken by various countries with regard to trading and investing in cryptocurrencies.

So, a question like 'Is the cryptocurrency market a good place to invest?' becomes ludicrous.

It is similar to asking whether the stock market is a good place to invest.

Investing in stocks can be very profitable. But it is possible that in some shares you may make losses, while in others you could make money.

Even if cryptocurrencies are here to stay, what we don't know is, if bitcoin is the right currency to invest in or are some of the altcoins, like Ethereum, Ripple, Litecoin, Dash, Monero are better bets.

Bitcoin is the first, and still the dominant, cryptocurrency. However, with the introduction of Altcoins in 2017, its share of the whole cryptomarket has fallen from 90 to around 40 per cent.

That said, Altcoins are somewhat harder to acquire. Some major exchanges like Kraken, BitFinex, and BitStamp, have started to list some popular Altcoins, like Litecoin, Ethereum, Monero, and Ripple.

'It is good to have money and the things that money can buy, but it's good too, to check up once in a while and make sure you haven't lost the things that money can't buy.'

George Horace Lorimer

Chapter 13

Should Home Loan Be Prepaid?

I have often been asked this question by people who have taken long-term housing loans.

After a few years of having paid the EMIs they are now in possession of surplus funds owing to increments in income, past savings or a windfall. The question they want answered is whether this money should be used to fully or partially prepay the housing loan, or should it be invested elsewhere.

The answer to this poser lies in a combination of factors that will need to be taken into account. These include the borrowers' financial status, temperament, risk-taking ability, other investment opportunities available, the state of the economy and the ability to do a cost-benefit analysis.

Reduction in tenure of the EMI

A housing loan is typically a long-term loan, usually carrying a rate of interest ranging from 8 to 11 per cent, with both the interest as well as the principal repayment enjoying income-tax deduction and providing tax relief to the borrower.

Each instalment of loan repaid reduces the principal sum outstanding and accordingly the interest component also comes down when calculated on a reducing balance method. As a result, the amount to be paid is successively lower with the passage of time.

However, in the case of housing loans, the repayment of the principal amount and the interest payable thereon are most often converted into an EMI, with the amount to be paid being constant throughout the tenure of the loan.

Consequently, the EMIs in the initial years are interest-heavy, that is a large percentage of the EMI consists of interest and a meagre amount being adjusted towards loan repayment. Toward the latter years, the reverse is the case with the bulk of the component being towards principal repayment and a smaller amount constituting interest.

This does not matter for loans that run their entire tenure. However, those who repay the loan in the first few years after availing it find that despite having paid a substantial amount back to the housing finance company, most of the principal sum of the loan is still outstanding and prepayment in such cases does not help as much.

This however may not be entirely true owing to the fact that the amount prepaid can go towards reducing the principal sum outstanding, and after such payment the interest burden would reduce. If the borrower continues to pay the same EMI, the loan would get repaid earlier than scheduled. Else the borrower can choose to keep the tenure the same as before and the prepayment would lead to a reduction in the amount of the EMI.

Therefore, the decision to prepay should be based on the prevailing interest rates and other investment opportunities available.

One should also take into account the charges for prepayment of the loan that the bank levies.

Helps reduce stress

Some people are temperamentally uncomfortable with a large housing loan looming over their heads. They may want to get rid of the loan burden at the earliest to reduce stress.

Some people are temperamentally uncomfortable with a large housing loan looming over their heads. They may want to get rid of the loan burden at the earliest to reduce stress. This could be out of a fear of losing the income stream due to loss of job, or an indisposition of the income earner on account of serious illness or even untimely passing away.

(Of course, it is possible to manage such risks by taking appropriate insurance policies for exactly such an eventuality).

Discontinuance of the tax deductions

If the home loan is not giving you sleepless nights, and the monthly income is sufficient to pay the EMI, it makes sense to continue with the regular instalment schedule. Currently, the principal component of the EMI is treated as investment under Section 80C. The interest component is also deducted from your taxable income under Section 24. The deduction in respect of the interest component of a housing loan, for a self-occupied house, is restricted to Rs 2 lakh per annum. So, for those paying interest in excess of Rs 2 lakh annually, it makes sense to prepay the loan, and save on future interest payment.

However, in case the loan has been taken on a joint name, the spouse being the co-borrower, the tax benefit for interest payment can double to Rs 4 lakh provided the joint holders share the EMIs.

Amount for a rainy day

Another argument in favour of not retiring the home loan and keeping it invested in liquid assets is the sense of security it provides of being able to access it in case of any emergency or other unexpected expenses that may arise.

Cost-benefit analysis

When prepaying a home loan, there are two things you must look at:
1) The saving in interest on account of prepayment and
2) Other avenues of investment that are available and the returns that can be generated.

One should opt for prepayment of the loan only if the after-tax returns on investment are greater than the effective rate of interest on the housing loan. If the latter is higher, don't.

The net-of-tax rate of interest on a housing loan works out to be pretty low. Many mutual fund schemes have been fetching returns that are far higher. Besides there are other risk-free investment opportunities also available like the PPF, NSCs, NPS and even certain tax-free bonds. And those who are not risk-averse and are familiar with the functioning of the stock market can earn even more significant returns.

It must be obvious that there is no straight answer to this question and the choice to be made would vary from situation to situation. A decision should be taken by each individual after weighing all the factors discussed here.

'About the time we can make the ends meet, somebody moves the ends.'

Herbert Clark Hoover

Chapter 14

Money Market Mutual Funds

Money market refers to a market where financial instruments with high liquidity and short-term maturities are traded.

These are debt and monetary instruments that are deemed to be close substitutes for money and they aid in the money exchange carried out in the primary and secondary market.

Broadly speaking, the money market is a marketplace where money is bought and sold.

Money market securities are issued by governments, financial institutions and large corporations. Just as in capital markets investments having long maturity are traded, large institutions and the government use the money market to manage their short-term cash needs.

Money markets facilitate the lending and borrowing of short-term funds, which are usually ranging in duration from overnight to one year. Short maturity period and high liquidity are two characteristic features of the instruments which are traded in the money market.

Since the maturity of these securities is generally below one year, this market is also called the cash market. This maturity differentiates money market from fixed-income market which consists of securities having a life of between one to five years.

Money market deals are not carried out in money/cash, but other instruments like trade bills, government papers, and promissory notes. Also, money market transactions cannot be done via brokers but have to be carried out via mediums like formal documentation, oral or written communication.

These instruments are also considered extremely safe.

The money market is a part of the larger financial market and consists of numerous smaller sub-markets like:

1. Call money market
2. Repurchase agreement (Repo & Reverse Repo) market
3. Treasury bill market
4. Commercial bill market
5. Commercial paper market
6. Certificates of deposit market
7. Money Market Mutual Fund (MMMF)
8. Cash Management Bill (CMB)

I will skip discussing details of each of the above, since the transactions are for large denominations and take place between financial institutions and companies rather than individuals.

So far as individuals are concerned, an opportunity to invest in these instruments is provided through money market mutual funds (MMMFs) that offer individuals the option to invest smaller amounts in these assets.

A money market fund is an open-ended mutual fund that invests in short-term debt securities such as treasury bills and commercial paper. These funds invest money in high-quality and very short maturity-based money market instruments.

These funds are widely regarded as being as safe as bank deposits, yet providing a higher yield.

When interest rates are down, money market securities could be pricey. This leads to these funds having a higher NAV at which an investor will have to buy them.

Taking a call on the future interest rates, demand for credit in the market and policies of the Reserve Bank of India (RBI) could be used as a guide to decide when to invest in MMMFs and when to liquidate them.

As individuals, having a diversified portfolio is desirable and making MMMFs part of one's portfolio should bring the overall risk down. Care, however, must be taken to ensure to enter at the right time, when these funds could be more revenue-adding to the portfolio.

‘A man wants to earn money in order to be happy, and his whole effort and the best of a life are devoted to the earning of that money. Happiness is forgotten; the means are taken for the end.’

Albert Camus

Chapter 15

Final Thoughts

Each person's portfolio is after all a personal choice.

A combination of factors goes into its composition, not the least being the personality traits and temperament of the individual. Besides, knowledge about different avenues of investment, risk-taking ability, family background, domestic responsibilities, certainty of the income stream and several other factors play an important role in moulding one's approach to personal finance.

Having said that, it would be a pity if certain investment opportunities are not exploited for want of knowledge or information about it.

This book has been written with a view to introducing certain concepts and principles required to be understood in order to take intelligent personal finance decisions and to expose you to some, though not all, investment options.

Let me list out a few finance management mantras that you must try and follow:

1. Inculcate the habit of saving early in life. I have said it before, let me reiterate. One of the most important things that you can do as an investor is to get an early start on investing. The old saying 'the early bird gets the worm,' is apt in this context.

If you are past that age, inculcate this habit in your children.

Investing early on in life is certainly not easy since the means at one's disposal are limited. But as Theodore Roosevelt famously said to 'Do what you can, where you are, with what you've got.'

The biggest advantage of doing so is you get to harness the power of compounding. In the words of Vanguard, compounding is 'the snowball effect that happens when your earnings generate even more earnings. You receive interest not only on your original investments but also on any interest, dividends and capital gains that accumulate, so your money can grow faster and faster as the years roll on.'

2. Invest in income-generating assets. The assets you accumulate over time can be divided into two types: performing and non-performing assets, that is, those that generate an income and those that lie idle. Try and invest in assets that have the potential to generate income.

3. A certain portion of your investments should be to meet short-term needs; a bigger portion should be for long-term purposes. Short-term investments should be income-generating and long-term should be appreciating assets.

4. Before spending, evaluate the options available and take financially intelligent decisions.

A friend of mine recently narrated this anecdote to me.

Five years ago, he purchased a high-end music system costing about Rs 200,000 that he had his eye on for some time.

Around the same time his brother, about four years younger than him, acquired a plot of land at Lonavala (a hill station near Pune) for a similar amount.

Today that plot of land is worth about Rs 2 crore. And the music system, well, it stopped working a couple of years ago.

5. Have a diversified portfolio but not too diversified. If you spread yourself too thin, it is difficult to monitor your investment.

6. Don't be too risk-averse. After securing yourself for the short-term future, it may not be a bad idea to stick your neck out a bit. Safe investments will never give you phenomenal returns. Remember risk and return have an inverse relationship. Once your basic needs are met and the immediate foreseeable future is secure, you can afford to take some risks. Besides people choose investments on grounds of safety when they do not understand anything about safety except its spelling.

Relatively riskier but lucrative investments include investment in stocks and shares. Invest in shares directly or through mutual funds.

However, always keep one principle in mind—it doesn't matter how attractive an investment proposal is, or what anyone says, by doing so if it is going to take away your sleep, don't do it.

This is personal finance and not business finance.

As Tim Maurer says, 'Personal finance . . . is more personal than it is finance.'

William Bruce Cameron has said, 'Not everything that can be counted counts and not everything that counts can be counted.' (This quote is often attributed to Albert Einstein).

Own a house, no matter what anyone says.

Take a home loan, if need be (even though I'm completely against taking loans in your personal life, the only exception I would make is in the case of a housing loan).

At this point in time, the real estate market appears to be lacklustre and it does make financial sense to live in a rented accommodation rather than owning it. However in the long-run property prices always rise. And what better time to make a long-term investment than when the market is perhaps at its lowest.

Invest in property through REITs, if not directly.

Keep a small amount of liquid cash at hand.

Invest some funds in easy-to-liquidate assets including a bit of gold.

Invest in assets/schemes/properties that can give a regular stream of alternative income in addition to your primary source of earning.

Take out an insurance policy of an adequate sum (including term plans) to protect your loved ones.

Get adequate medical insurance and free yourself from the stress and financial trauma arising from unforeseen illnesses or mishaps.

Invest in tax-saving instruments like a PPF scheme, ELSS or NPS.

Devote a certain portion of your time to managing your money.

Take charge of your personal finance management. Your level of success in life depends on your level of financial intelligence.